WHY DO CATS SULK?

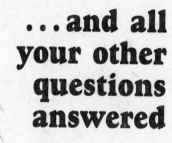

...and all your other questions answered

researched &
written by
Arline
Bleecker

Contents

Introduction

God made the cat in order to give man the
pleasure of petting the tiger.
Anonymous

Over the last 15 years, my husband and I have shared our household with over a dozen cats, and each one entered our lives in a different way.

The first was Val, a regal and commanding Russian Blue – full-grown, near death, and almost frozen to the bone when a friend found him in New York City. His arrival marked the beginning of my love affair with cats.

Val was quickly followed by Pepper. Within a year of adopting Pepper, she disappeared for 10 days, was crushed by a car, then dragged herself back home with her uninjured front paws. She could easily have been given up for dead, yet the vet was optimistic – reassuring us that Pepper hadn't made it all the way home just to die. Fourteen years later, Pepper is still with us – limp, deaf as a post, and as lovable as ever.

Pepper's greatest gift to us was her offspring we called Blueberry – named by a friend who said her calico fur looked like vanilla ice cream melting over blueberry pie.

Perhaps the most unexpected addition to our family came from the stray carrot-colored cat we initially named Morris. Morris, you see, turned out to be Marie! We never even knew she was pregnant until her single white kitten was born.

No matter how many strays turn up at my door, I can honestly say I never met a cat I didn't love. Eventually, our menagerie included Bucky and Tam, TC and Red, Mutton

Chops and Kitten. One of our adoptees was a three-week-old kitten we scooped from a flooded drain. Naturally, we named him Moses.

There was the silver tabby who leapt from nowhere onto my shoulder on a crowded Florida beach. There was the kitten we discovered on a golf course; a wounded black cat who was just minutes from being put to sleep; and finally, Little Guy, a plume-tailed long-hair whose amber eyes peered soulfully at me from the bushes one afternoon and who now reigns as Top Cat in our current five-cat household.

As a writer, I'm lucky to work at home, among this ceaselessly intriguing and amazing furry brood. I never tire of watching them, and I still get a thrill knowing they're just a whisker away from their jungle ancestors.

They are creatures of eternal enchantment. Their agile bodies are fascinating and challenging to watch. Author and artist Peter Warner in his book *Perfect Cats* calls them "life paintings with fur on." In an instant, they can go from a tranquil, resting state to furious hunter – all the while maintaining their grace and beauty. They are charming creatures, at the same time very aware of their surroundings, yet seemingly not caring at all.

Frankly, I don't know whether all dog people can recognize other dog people, but I always seem to know another cat lover. And cat lovers, I'm convinced, are made, not born. Once committed, they can't wait to turn on the whole world to the mysterious world of the cat.

Though I've lived among them for 15 years, these alluring creatures still seem to pose more questions than answers. I'm still asking them, and I'm sure the same is true for you.

Here are some that may fascinate you...

The Mind

If you would know what a cat is
thinking about, you must hold its paw in
your hand for a long time...
Jules Champfleury

Why do cats sulk?

Try to imagine the world through a cat's eyes. From way down there on the ground, everything looks pretty big – huge, in fact.

Just imagine how big you look to her – especially when you scold her. It isn't what you say so much as how you say it. The poor little thing becomes so intimidated, she just turns her back and refuses – under any condition – to look at you.

You may think she is sulking; perhaps even punishing you. But actually it's her way of withdrawing. In order to tone down the threat of hostility from this gigantic creature (meaning you), she's really only avoiding eye contact.

When you look down at your cat as you discipline her, she associates your fixed gaze with 'the enemy'. In hostile situations, the dominant cat always stares at her rival, who looks away rather than risk increasing the hostility. When you stare at your cat (especially in an angry way), you become the dominant rival... and, let's face it, you're much bigger and scarier. So when she turns away, she isn't sulking; she has simply surrendered.

For many animals, eyes are a signal of power with which to intimidate an enemy. Nature has even lent a helping hand. In comparison to your cat's size, for instance, her eyes are enormous.

Why won't my cat come when I call her?

There's an old joke that goes something like this:

When you call a dog, he comes right over to you. When you call a cat, she takes a message and maybe, just *maybe*, she'll get back to you later.

More likely, your cat doesn't answer your call because she's off somewhere snoozing. And, although you think it's important for her to come running (a trip to the vet, bath time, dinner, etc.), she doesn't see any reason to stop what *she's* doing.

Why does your cat interrupt when you're on the phone?

You know the drill: You're on the phone and here comes Kitty. She leaps to the table, rubs her face all over yours, insists you rub her back, all the while, disrupting your conversation.

You gently set her onto the floor but, in a flash, she's back at it again. This yo-yo-ing – up and down, up and down – goes on and on, over and over, but she never seems to get the point.

This weird behavior is not her deliberate attempt to be a part of your telephone call, or because she's jealous that you're talking to someone else. In fact, she doesn't even have the slightest idea that you are talking to someone else. She hasn't got a clue that there's someone on the other end of the line – she actually thinks you're talking to her!

You're probably speaking in soft, melodic tones, and that's what Kitty is responding to. (A business call is less likely to result in this behavior.)

Why do cats always run to the one person in the room who doesn't like cats?

To understand the reason, it helps to remember that cats see us as huge and intimidating creatures.

When Kitty enters a room full of people, what she actually sees is a room full of other cats – except they're all larger and louder than she is. All these people-cats start staring at Kitty, saying how beautiful and graceful she is. All this staring makes Kitty very uncomfortable. Then she spies the only person-cat in the room who's not staring at her – the person who doesn't like cats. He or she is quiet, looking in the opposite direction, hoping that Kitty will look away and go to someone else.

But Kitty is feeling intimated by all those stares, so she seeks out a safe lap. The only one in the room not moving, not waving their hands, not meowing and not staring is the cat-hater. Kitty makes a beeline right for him or her.

Here's a hint for non-cat-lovers (since they probably aren't reading this book, you'll have to tell them): When you're in a room with a cat, pretend you *like* her!

What makes cats purr?

When my cats purr, I'm never sure who's happier – them or me. The sound is so soothing, it's almost hypnotic.

Cats (big and small) are the only animals that purr. "Why?" is one of the most frequently asked questions when it comes to cats. Purring isn't 'speaking', it's even more mysterious. The purr comes from two membrane folds, called false vocal cords, that are situated in the larynx behind the actual vocal cords. Cats purr at 26 cycles per second, the same as an idling diesel engine. Kitty purrs both when she inhales and exhales, all the time keeping her mouth completely closed.  Scientists think purring is produced by blood in a large vein in the chest cavity that vibrates and is then magnified by air in the windpipe.

You can actually feel the vibration – just like newborn kittens do. Kittens are born blind and deaf; but the vibration of their mother's purring is a physical signal that the kittens can feel – it acts like a homing device, signaling them to nurse. Kittens begin purring at about one week old, and it's a signal back to Mom that they're getting their milk and are content. Since purring is non-vocal, it doesn't interfere with the kitten's sucking. What an ingenious survival tool!

Now we all know that cats purr when they're happy – eyes closed almost all the way and wearing what almost looks like a smile. But contrary to what most of us think, cats don't just purr for pleasure. Be alert: A deep purr can indicate that your feline is in pain or distress. Female cats, for instance, purr when they're in labor. Sometimes cats purr from fear -- like a visit to the vet. For example, when my Pepper found her way home after being hit by a car, she was purring!

Cats will also purr when they're anticipating something that will make them happy – like thinking they're going to get fed or stroked.

Big African cats only purr in short bursts, but your kitty can purr for hours. Curiously, a cat never purrs when she's alone . . . (Hmmmm, I wonder how we know that?)

Why are cats so curious?

Sarcastically advising a friend who wanted to get rid of his cat, humorist Dorothy Parker quipped: "Have you tried curiosity?"

Parker apparently wasn't a cat lover, or she'd never have offered such advice!

Cats are perhaps the most curious animals around, but they can get into a whole lot of trouble because of it. By nature, the cat is an explorer and is constantly on the hunt. So part of the reason for their curiosity is that they're always looking for food.

Some 'hunts' don't end up all that successful. In 1986, one curious cat got shut in a fridge for 12 hours. Victa was pronounced dead by a vet but suddenly stood up and walked away. Hundreds of such tales just reinforce our amazement at their curious curiosity.

Do cats dream?

They sure do. And it's probably a happy dream of catching a yummy mouse or two.

Just like humans, cats alternate phases of deep and light sleep. Dreaming occurs during the deep-sleep phase (ours is called REM sleep, for Rapid Eye Movement). During a cat's deep-sleep phase, the giveaway to the "Do-they-dream?" mystery is that they move their paws and claws, twitch their whiskers and flick their ears. Sometimes they even vocalize. My little calico sleeps so soundly, she actually snores. But even though they seem dead to the world while sleeping, don't assume that they are: They can spring to life in a millisecond. Believe me, I've tried it. I have the scratches to prove it!

Why do cats' tails quiver?

A cat's tail tells many tales. When the tip of her tail is quivering, it can mean mild irritation. But if the tail is erect – and the whole length of it seems to be quivering with joy or excitement – that's exactly what she's trying to tell you. It's definitely a friendly quiver. You probably notice this kind of fluttering occurs when you've come home after being away awhile. Can the can opener be far behind?

Why do they 'swish' their tails?

Veterinarian Jim Grubb hazards a guess. Actually, he offers two possibilities: One reason, he says, is to get their balance before leaping – like building up a head of steam or cranking up the engine for those flying leaps; and two, to mesmerize the 'prey' they're looking at. Since your kitty can't see prey if the prey 'freezes', she moves her tail to initiate the slightest movement in her target, which she can then spot. Pretty smart, eh?

What does it mean when she 'lashes' her tail from side to side?

The tail waving quietly from side to side is a sure sign of contentment; and if she sits quietly with her tail gently wagging back and forth, she's concentrating intently on something. But vigorous lashing back and forth is a clear sign of anger. It signals annoyance, and it's a good sign that she's very upset. If she's lashing her tail while you're stroking or petting her – back off. She's sending a clear signal that she's had enough, even of your affectionate attention. She'll use a whole lot of different signals to express her anger – but she's nice enough to warn you first with her lashing tail. If you persist, she may begin to growl. Her ultimate move could be attack.

A tail-wagging tempo that falls somewhere between heavy-duty and halfhearted can mean your cat feels very indecisive. She may want to go out, for instance, then realizes it's raining. She'll wag her tail because she's torn between wanting to go out and not wanting to get wet. As soon as she makes up her mind, the wagging will stop.

What else can 'tails tell'?

When her tail is bent forward over her head, it means she's feeling like top cat; when she waves it quietly from side to side like a lady's fan, she's contented; several quick flicks upward is a greeting – both for you and other cats.

What do the different ear positions mean?

Almost as many different things as her tail does. There are five basic ear signals, revealing if your cat is feeling relaxed, alert, agitated, defensive or aggressive.

When her ears point forward and slightly outward, she is

relaxed and carefully listening to everything that's going on. When they're erect and facing forward, she's alert and ready to investigate a noise she's heard.

When they twitch nervously back and forth, she is agitated or anxious. If she's watching something closely – like that bird she's forever fascinated by – her ear twitching will probably be accompanied by two quick flicks of her tongue around her lips.

When she flattens her ears tightly against her head, she's signaling annoyance and is feeling defensive. A cat will pin her ears back to protect herself during a fight.

When she's feeling aggressive (but not frightened) she'll put her ears at half-mast – in a position somewhere between alert and defensive.

What can we tell about a cat's behavior from her fur?

Like most other parts of your cat's remarkable body, even her hair is a mirror of her moods.

When she's a scaredy-cat – alarmed by the sudden crash of a crystal bowl she just broke – her hair will stand up on end all over her body. When she feels threatened, however – when another cat is about to attack her, for example – her hair stands up only in a narrow band along her spine and on her tail. The hair also will incline slightly toward the middle from both sides, and forms a sharp ridge. This is nature's way of making her appear larger than she is to her enemies.

Can we read anything in their whiskers?

Well . . . it's not quite the same as tea leaves. But a cat's whiskers contribute to your cat's facial expressions. Depending on how they're positioned or spread out, whiskers can reveal many things about your cat's moods:

When they're pointed forward and fanned out, it means your cat is tense. Not nervous necessarily, but alert, excited and ready to act. My fluffy Little Guy's whiskers look this way whenever he's feeling especially affectionate and is asking to be cuddled. When a cat bunches her whiskers together and flattens them to the side of her face, she's feeling reserved, timid or even shy. When they point sideways and are not terribly spread out, your cat is comfortable, calm, relaxed, friendly, satisfied – or just indifferent.

Why do cats arch their backs?

To anyone with a back problem, the mere sight of a cat arching its back into an inverted 'U' isn't just amazing, it's downright enviable!

The cat's arching back is actually part of her complex body-language system. The arched back usually is accompanied by her hair standing out all over her body, especially on her tail. This is your kitty's response to feeling threatened. Sometimes, she'll even turn sideways to present an even more impressive profile in order to scare away a threatening animal. The arch is able to get so high because her spine contains nearly 60 vertebrae (we humans only have about 34) which fit together loosely, giving her that incredible flexibility.

Why do cats suddenly take off at 90 miles an hour?

Actually, it's 31 miles per hour.

One cat observer calls this familiar mad dash the 'frantic

tarantella'. Whatever name it goes by in your household, we're all well acquainted with that spook-induced racing from one end of the room to the other. At full tilt, they clock an amazing 31 mph and cover about three times their own length per leap. (Cheetahs, which are the fastest land animals, hit their stride at around 70 mph).

This behavior is a result of pent-up energy that suddenly overflows. Remember, our kitties are nocturnal beings and natural hunters.

The sedentary lifestyle imposed on an indoor cat literally can drive her stir crazy. The result is this nighttime frenzy of activity.

Sometimes only the smallest noise triggers this massive reaction. Even in an environment where there's nothing to hunt – and your kitty no longer even needs to hunt – these creatures who still have one paw in the jungle, feel the need to hunt anyway.

What does it mean when your cat does that unusual little 'hop'?

You've seen the routine a hundred times: Kitty zips over to you, bumps against your leg, quickly lifts both front paws off the ground together and puts them down again. That familiar little hop-like greeting is generally reserved just for humans.

It's your cat's way of saying 'welcome', and it's actually a throwback to the head-to-head greeting behavior she learned from her own Mom.

In your cat's mind, you've replaced her real Mom, so you get the same greeting...sort of. Kitty's real Mom would lower her own head to make face-to-face contact and rub noses with her in order to mingle scents. But since you're so tall, and Kitty's so short, she settles for what she can get.

Doesn't that make you feel special?

18

Why will a cat rub up against your leg?

When she rubs her head or the side of her chin against you – or against the furniture, or the trees or other cats or, for that matter, just about anything – she's actually depositing her scent on objects she considers part of her territory. It's as if she's saying, "This is mine."

Like it or not, you're one of her possessions.

To anoint you with her special scent, she uses glands on her forehead and around her mouth and chin. These glands produce chemicals called pheromones, which she transfers by rubbing against you.

You should be grateful for the rubbing: Your cat could choose to 'mark' her territory by spraying it with urine, a powerful scent picked up by other cats – and anyone else with a nose! Experts say cats can tell just how long ago a scent was laid down and just how much they need to pay attention to the warning.

Why does a cat roll over and show her stomach?

This is a rare form of greeting – and the ultimate compliment. It indicates complete trust. If your cat could talk, she'd say, "I trust you completely." Instead, she uses her body language to show how much she loves you and how comfortable she is around you.

Totally exposing her stomach reveals how secure she feels, because lying in this position exposes her most vulnerable part – and she knows it.

Sometimes, she may just be asking for a caress by flopping down this way; sometimes it means she's asking you to play; sometimes she may just want that tender tummy stroked. But sleeping on her back is another matter entirely, her trust in you is in the stratosphere!

Why do cats chase birds?

Because they can.

Your little carnivore Kitty is just a bundle of instincts, and it probably isn't news to you that she'll play with anything that moves. She is, after all, a huntress! Never mind that the 'prey' is just a nutrition-less, tasteless sock. She's still doing what comes naturally.

One of my cats can be entertained (and exercised) for hours trying to catch an evasive circle of light from a flashlight that I reflect onto the wall. Of course, I'm in an easy chair.

Why do cats act as if they were born to be stroked?

Because in their minds, they were.

Cats carry many of their memories of kittenhood into adulthood; it's almost as if they never grew up.

They respond to our stroking, for example, because they see us as their mothers; and they interpret our stroking as if they were being groomed by their real Mom's tongue – just like when they were kittens.

Why do cats 'knead' when they're happy?

Here's another example of cats retaining memories of kittenhood.

That loud purring followed by her sharpening her claws on some soft spot on your body is called 'milk-treading'. When you relax and sit quietly, you're unwittingly giving your cat the same signal she got from her mother when she was a kitten – that Mom was ready to let her suckle.

A nursing kitten instinctively uses her paws to draw out the milk, gently pushing her mother's stomach to increase the flow. When older cats behave this way, it's a good sign that they're happy and content, and very likely are recalling the best days of their lives.

Why do cats get stuck in trees?

Actually, we only think they do. As a vet friend of mine points out, we've never seen a cat skeleton in a tree. Eventually, they all come down. Until then, their pitiful caterwauling seems designed to turn us – and our local fire departments – into emergency feline rescuers.

So how come they're up there in the first place? Simple.

Their claws are constructed for climbing up. The problem is, because their claws curve the wrong way – it's almost impossible for them to climb down.

If you're patient enough, though, Kitty will eventually figure out how to do it – slowly shimmying backward as her claws cling (the right way!) to the tree bark.

I once found my cat, TC, dangling from a tree branch by just the claws of her two front paws. She clung on for dear life – looking somewhat like a Christmas tree ornament – for what seemed like hours (though it was merely min-

utes) before finally deciding to jump to the ground. Don't be terribly disturbed if it takes your cat all night to figure out a solution.

Why does Kitty 'torture' her prey?

Your cat's hunting technique is a mixed marvel of cunning and skill. But because it often looks like a sport or a game, we see it as cruel.

Field cats – who actually live off their catch – will kill and eat what they catch immediately. Your domestic cat's hunting expeditions, however, are hardly ever related to hunger. Thanks to you, she no longer needs to hunt to eat; yet she still has a strong need to keep her natural hunting skills in good working order.

So she hunts, but she doesn't kill. She probably never was instructed by her mother on the finer points of cat dining. It's very likely that she has no idea she's supposed to eat this poor creature.

And Kitty doesn't know how to inflict that 'killing bite'. That's the reason she seems so wishy-washy about the whole process. If cats haven't been taught by their mothers to kill swiftly, they aren't likely to pick up this hunting skill themselves.

Why does a cat bury her mess?

When you consider that she is evolved from desert animals, it's pretty easy to understand why she buries her mess in the sand.

Many experts, however, suggest that cats bury their feces in the first place because they're so fussy. While it's true that they are pretty picky characters, they don't bury their waste products because of fastidiousness alone.

In the wild, only secondary cats bury them; the dominant feline, on the other hand, will actually display its feces prominently. This sends a strong message of its dominance.

However, in today's modern home, you are the dominant animal – and Kitty chooses not to offend you. House cats will carefully bury their feces to eliminate interfering with what they perceive as the natural order, says Gary Brodsky in *The Mind of the Cat*. Another explanation is just as logical: Like most animals, cats bury their waste to protect their trail from predators.

Whatever the real reason, let's be grateful for the reality. It sure beats having to walk your cat!

Why do cats like to hang out and sleep in high places?

The answer is simple: Just about anything up high gives them a great view from which to keep an eye on their property. It's safe and secure, and they can keep a watchful look-out for prey.

In the case of your housebound kitty, of course, that means perching atop your fridge to ensure she'll be nearby when you haul out that can of ground-up, store-bought 'prey'.

Do cats have a memory?

You can easily test this one out yourself: See if yours remembers the sound of a can opener.

You get the point?!

Your cat's memory can be up to 200 times more retentive than a dog's. But Kitty uses her memory only for what she regards as useful functions – and usually only what suits her.

Her memory is quite selective. Remember that 'second' visit to the vet? And isn't it amazing how well she remembers her name at mealtimes? She's also bound to remember that her human housemate opened the front door for her yesterday, and the day before, and the day before that. But she'll never quite remember *not* to scratch the furniture or stretch out on that black angora sweater.

Why does a cat quiver her jaw when she sees a bird?

We really don't know the answer to this one. That odd behavior that resembles teeth-chattering is usually produced when your cat sees something she wants, but can't get to – like a fly on the wall or a bird outside the window.

24

And even though her mouth is open slightly, her lips are pulled back, jaw opening and closing rapidly, it's not really considered an attempt at communication. The noise she makes is a combination of her lip-smacking and teeth-chattering as she gets more excited. She may even emit small bleating noises like a baby goat. But so far, none of this is believed to have any function.

Speaking of noise, what exactly is caterwauling?

The dictionary defines it simply as 'quarreling noisily'. I suspect the dictionary writer never owned a cat!

To anyone who's ever had to endure these ear-splitting sounds – which invariably shatter your night's sleep – caterwauling ranks right up there with fingernails on a blackboard.

Tomcats take most of the blame, but every cat I've ever lived with has taken a turn – male or female, neutered or not.

Someone has even had the nerve to suggest caterwauling is a tomcat's love song. That's not even close. It is, without a doubt, a 'song' of threat and war. Rival cats will emit these wailing sounds as they approach each other.

Why does a cat hiss and spit when attacked or threatened?

Maybe they're expressing an opinion about that awful caterwauling. (Just kidding.)

Actually, the truth is even funnier. Believe it or not, they're imitating snakes. The sound of a cat's hiss is almost the same sound a snake makes – and a snake is one of the most feared animals there is. Hissing is pretty common in all land animals. When your kitty hisses, she opens her mouth halfway, draws back her upper lip and wrinkles her face. As

25

she does this, she expels her breath so hard that, if you were close enough, you could feel the jet of air.

The moisture she releases with this gusty breath is what we call spitting.

And it seems to work rather well. It's as if the hiss is cat language for "This is absolutely my final warning before I rip you to ribbons!" It almost always succeeds in repulsing an enemy.

Cats are so fearful of being hissed at that yours probably will shy away if you blow into her face or merely open a soda pop bottle near her.

Why does your cat always want to be out when she's in ... and in when she's out?

Your cat has a powerful need to check out her territory from time to time. And though she adores making these repeated inspections, she never wants to spend too much time on it.

The reason her checking is so rhythmic is because of the built-in time clock of her scent marks. When she's outside, she rubs a territory marker or sprays urine on it to keep rivals away.

But the staying-power of this scent becomes weaker with time, and eventually disappears. This means she needs another visit outside to do it all over again. Once this is done, she's ready to trot back in again to the warmth and security of your cozy home.

In the wild, she could come and go as she pleased. In your house, however, the door stands in her way. And it doesn't take her too long to figure out that you're her solution to the door problem.

A cat door with a flap can help. Until then, you're it!

Why are cats territorial?

All cats are territorial by nature, even those who live indoors. They're very protective of their space – and heaven help the intruder!

Inside your home, Kitty claims just about everything as her own – from an entire room to a specific corner of your bed.

Outdoors, though, it's especially important for her to stake her territorial claim. It could be nothing more than your back yard; or it could be quite large – limited only by how big an area your cat feels she can reasonably defend. New cats in a neighborhood have to fight to be accepted and to win territory.

Your cat establishes territory for the same reasons you live in your home or apartment: She needs a safe place for sleeping, eating and relaxing.

Each cat's territory includes a few different kinds of spaces: private (for Kitty only, where she can sleep and feel safe), commonly held grounds (which she will share with a few other cats) and meeting grounds (where a group of cats will meet). There's also an outer part of her territory, where she can hunt and roam.

One way or another – usually by battling it out – cats establish their own territories. Often, they'll form a 'time-share' system, using the same areas but at different times. When they fail to agree on the rules, the caterwauling begins.

Why do cats feel compelled to bring that dead mouse into the house?

As with any hunter, returning with the spoils of the hunt is your cat's way of proudly bringing you back a present. Accept the gift gratefully – at least she doesn't expect you to eat it!

Just why cats bring in their prey isn't known for sure. In the wild, big cats do it as a social gesture. Perhaps they prefer to eat it in the safety of their den where chances of theft are pretty slim.

House cats present prey to their owners in an effort to introduce them to the concept of hunting, says Desmond Morris in *Catwatching*. Normally, cats see us as a parent figure; but when they present us with their prey, they see us as their kittens. Consider it a compliment; then just throw it out when they're not looking.

Indoor cats don't have a lot of opportunity to exercise their hunting instincts. That means you'll have to tolerate the occasional catnip mouse or squeaky toy instead.

What do your cat's eyes reveal about her moods?

To humans, eyes have long been thought of as the window of our souls. While you can't really tell who your cat is from her eyes, they certainly are good clues to what she's thinking or feeling – tipping us off to a range of emotions.

The pupils of a hungry cat's eyes, for instance, will dilate up to five times their normal size when Kitty spies her food bowl – even if it's empty. They'll also appear as big black pools when she's frightened or threatened.

Don't overlook those eyelids, either: Half closed, they say she's totally relaxed; when they're fully closed, she's either very satisfied – or asleep! Your cat also will shut her eyes for protection against a dominant rival. When she feels forced into submission, she 'cuts off' the image of her tormentor. The victor perceives this as defeat and usually walks away.

In China, peasants tell time by looking at a cat's eyes, which dilate and contract according to the sun's strength. The pupils are narrowest at noon.

Why are cats so tough to train?

No self-respecting cat would be caught dead playing dead. But even if your feline friend won't do flips through a fiery hoop, consider yourself fortunate: At least she's trained to use the litter box!

Actually, cat's aren't that tough to train – they just refuse to perform for a pat on the head. They're rather indifferent to the whole process, and learn tricks only when they want to. Because they're not renowned for their obedience, we think they're defiant. However, if there's something in it for them, no problem.

Basically, cats learn by association. Consider the cat carrier, for example: To her, the carrier is associated with a trip to the vet; and all you have to do is get it out of the garage and she vanishes. One of my cats who takes medication every day disappears when I go to the kitchen cabinet to fetch her pills. How she knows I'm going for her medication – and not for the ketchup or the salt – I'll never know. I do have a cat who fetches; but to be honest, I really think she trained me to play with her, not the other way 'round.

One of the reasons it seems so difficult to train cats is that you can't bribe them with sweets. Their taste buds don't have any sweet receptors (as meat-eaters they don't need them). In fact, they can't even tell the difference between a sugar solution and plain water.

As with all animals, coaxing them includes lots of love, patience, consistency, authority, repetition and reward – but never punishment.

I have a feeling that cats only lead us to believe they can't be trained, because they don't want to be bothered. Consider this comparison: Dogs are trainable because they're born to follow leaders. On the other hand, your cat can take care of herself.

How smart are cats?

According to Dr. David Greene, author of *Your Incredible Cat*, your cat may possess an IQ that is surpassed only in the animal kingdom by monkeys and chimps.

We know that cats think and adapt to changing circumstances, and that they learn by observation, imitation, and trial and error. If her Mom's a hunter, for example, the chances are pretty good that she will be, too. Interestingly, cats seem to learn more quickly from their own mothers than from examples set by unrelated cats.

It seems they can imitate humans, too. My entire brood has learned that the doorknob opens the door: They stare at it if they want to go in or out.

Evidence from lab experiments indicates that cats possess a high level of intelligence skills. Dr. Donald Adams has shown that cats can remember problem-solving strategies and that they use insight to think their way out of unusual situations.

Not that your cat is Harvard material, but they have been shown to exhibit greater problem-solving abilities than dogs. And tests conducted by the University of Michigan and the Department of Animal Behavior at the American Museum of Natural History concluded that while canine memory lasts no more than five minutes, cats' recall can last as long as sixteen hours – exceeding even that of monkeys and orangutans.

Do cats think?

Generally, a cat's intelligence is confined to cautiousness – with a guarded view of the world. They're smart enough to know danger, and remarkably well equipped to avoid it.

Their curiosity is related to their high intelligence, and they will work endlessly in order to get the results they want – food, for example. I once watched Pepper trying to open the kitchen cabinet where she knows her food is kept. She kept at it until she eventually managed to open it. She knocked the food box out of the closet, and happily nibbled away on the spillage. Cats seem to realize that it never does any harm to ask for what they want, but they will *never* work for work's sake.

Can cats read?

Personally, my cats aren't dog-earing any of my books. But a new book called *Teach Your Cat to Read* (Chronicle Books, 1-800-722-6657 $12.95) hopes to change all that.

With a hefty dose of humor, the book maintains that teaching your cat to read isn't as difficult as it sounds. That remains to be seen.

The package includes two paperback books, a red plastic alphabet-bordered feeding bowl and an assortment of props. Just fill the bowl with tasty cat grub, set up the attached easel, and prop the little books against it. Start with *The Cat's First Reader*, which opens with the word 'bird' on one side of the page and a large colorful illustration of a bird on the other. When your furry friend has gotten the essential vocabulary down, move her on to the *Advanced Cat's Reader*, complete with a cat dictionary and a list of books for further reading.

Kitty lit's never been easier.

The Body

A kitten is so flexible that she is almost
double; the hind parts are equivalent to
another kitten...She does not discover that
her tail belongs to her until you tread upon it.
Henry David Thoreau

Why do cats' eyes glow in the dark?

Cats' glow-in-the-dark eyes seem eerie, mystical, even scary when they pop out at you from the black of night – especially since your cat is one of only a few animals that can return a human's stare.

There is a simple explanation for that characteristic green or gold shine. A membrane, called *tapetum lucidum*, coats the eye and reflects light. When a cat is in the dark, her pupils open wide and light is reflected off them, but they're not actually 'glowing'. This ability, along with their extraordinary sensitivity to ultraviolet rays, enables them to see so well in the dark.

Can cats really see in the dark?

They can't see in total darkness – and their daytime vision is only fair. But they can see better than humans in semi-darkness. They also can distinguish brightness seven times better than we can.

As nocturnal hunters, their eyes are able to scoop up even the smallest scrap of available light. Their vision generally is blurred at the edges and they see best at six to 20 feet. When it comes to movement, though, your cat doesn't miss a twitch.

By the way, feeding dog food to your cat is a no-no. Dog food lacks *taurine,* a substance crucial for your cat's eyesight. A diet without it will make your cat go blind.

Do cats see in color?

It once was believed cats were colorblind, but now we know they actually can tell the difference between certain colors. Basically, they see the world around them as shades of blue and green. But though they see color, cats don't pay much attention to it. In nature, color isn't particularly necessary to a cat's survival success.

Why do all tabbies have an 'M' on their foreheads?

Since most of the world's cats are tabbies, that distinctive 'M' – which is part of the fur pattern and clearly seen on Morris the Cat – is a genetic feature passed on from generation to generation. But being the fascinating creatures that cats are, we've woven a myth around this physical feature.

An Italian legend believes a cat gave birth in the stable in Bethlehem at exactly the same moment Mary gave birth to Christ. As the Christ child lay in the manger, no animal could soothe him to sleep – not even the gentle donkey or the faithful shepherd dog. But when the little tabby jumped into the manger and began to purr, the infant responded as if to a lullaby and soon fell asleep. Ever since, the legend goes, all tabbies' foreheads have been marked with an 'M' as a symbol of the Madonna's gratitude.

Why do cats flick their ears when they're asleep?

A cat's remarkable ears each have 30 muscles that control the outer ear (by comparison, our ears only have six muscles). These muscles rotate 180 degrees, so she can hear without moving her head. Even though your snoozing kitty appears to sleep quite often, most of the time she's only dozing – and she's constantly searching the air for messages that might mean she needs to spring into action at the spur of the moment.

What's the purpose of that 'pad' midway up the rear of a cat's leg?

It does look pretty useless, I'll admit – sitting way up there on the back of the leg like that. But it does have a purpose. It's called the carpal pad, and it acts as an anti-skid insurance policy for crash landings (which, of course, are rare) or to keep your energetic kitty from hitting a wall as she speeds around the house like a race car.

Why does the Manx cat have no tail?

The absence of a tail in the Manx has led to several 'tall tales'. The most common legend says that the tail was lost because the Manx was late boarding the Ark and Noah accidentally slammed the door on her tail.

Actually, the Manx's lack of tail is a true genetic abnormality first observed in the 16th century. At that time, these mutant cats had been brought back from the Far East to the Isle of Man, off the coast of Britain, and the island's isolation led to myths about how their taillessness came about. It was said that the cats slipped and slid on their rear ends around the slippery rocks on the island and eventually erased all traces of their tails.

However amusing these tales are, the tail mutation is a serious defect. There's a hollow in the Manx's body where the tail should be; and this distorts the rest of the spine so that the Manx has a backbone with fewer and shorter vertebrae.

A true Manx is called a 'rumpy'; if she has a tiny tail, she's a 'stumpy'. The Manx is sometimes called a 'bunny' because her strong back legs are longer than her front legs. As a result, she runs with a hop.

What makes their tails so flexible?

Your cat's tail contains between 14 and 28 *caudal* or tail vertebrae, linked like a string of loosely threaded beads.

Even the tailless Manx has three tail vertebrae (although flexibility obviously isn't one of her strong suits). Short of a short tail, the Manx looks just like an ordinary cat.

Why do we say cats have three eyelids?

Although it sounds like a weird science fiction movie, those 'three' eyelids are really quite useful. The 'third' eyelid is actually that tiny triangle of pinkish or whitish tissue that is sometimes visible in the corner of your cat's eye. It's called the haw, or nictating membrane. Humans have something like it – that small pink lump at the inner corner of our eyes. However, in your cat, the haw will raise automatically and then move sideways across the eye to protect or lubricate its sensitive surface. If Kitty is in ill health, undernourished or is on the verge of catching a disease, the presence of the haw is a pretty good clue. The spontaneous 'movement' occurs because pads of fat behind the eyeballs – which act as shock absorbers – start to shrink when your animal is in poor health. Usually, it's a signal to get Kitty to a vet.

Why do cats shed?

For pretty much the same reason other animals do – it's their way of going from a winter wardrobe to their summer duds. That is, less hair means a cooler body. Cats lose more hair in summer because the increased light from longer days triggers the shedding process. The average house cat – lolling around under electric lights, or even near the light of a TV screen – also will shed more. Stress adds still another factor that will make them shed more swiftly.

Why do cats shed their claws?

Cats are the only animals that walk directly on their claws, not on their paws. It would be like humans walking on the tips of their fingers. Getting around on tip-toe – called *digitigrade* – is a particularly useful feature to have when it comes to moving at high speeds. Being the great hunter she is, the cat needs to keep this skill very sharp.

True, she may occasionally manicure her nails on your antique dresser but contrary to what you may think, it's not out of malice. Actually, it's really not even done to sharpen her claws. What she's actually doing when she's clawing your couch cushions to shreds is tearing off the ragged edges of the sheaths of her talons. All year long she sheds her claws to expose new sharp ones beneath.

Personally, I've never found a scratching post a solution to the clawing problem. For all the good it does, it may as well be an umbrella stand! But I do find that squirting the offender with a water mister when I catch her in the act does help. Problem is, I have to be on the spot when the deed is being done!

Nevertheless, I have never declawed any of my cats. Claws aren't just for Kitty's protection; they are responsible for your cat's exquisite balance and other amazing feats such as climbing, stretching and running and grooming. Declawing not only physically afflicts her, but she's also psychologically anguished, deprived of her only defense and one of her most versatile tools for survival.

Why do they sometimes retract their claws?

A cat pulls in her claws to protect them and to keep them sharp. They need to be kept sharp for all the reasons just explained. Cats also need sharp claws because they use them to help mark their territory. In the act of scratching, sweat glands between the paw pads secrete a scent transferred to the tree trunk or to your treasured table or sofa. This is how your cat identifies the scratched area as her own.

In the animal kingdom, your cat's retractable claws are her most unique feature. When she extends her legs, the paws automatically expand to an extraordinary size and the claws appear.

What makes cats so cute and cuddly?

Have you ever noticed that your cat is just about the same size as an infant? Case closed.

Actually, I didn't mean to answer a question with a question, but everything about your cat's body is a recipe for cuddling (that is, if she'll have it).

A cat has a toasty body temperature of 102 degrees. A good percentage of the nutrients she gets in her daily food intake (approximately 30 percent) is devoted to making her skin and coat supple and fuzzy. Stir in a spine that lets them curl up like a soft pretzel and, *voila,* you feel like you're holding an infant. Add a dollop of soft purring, and who could possibly pass up such a deliciously inviting opportunity?

Why do cats like to fall asleep in the sun?

Just like us, they prefer to feel warm and secure before falling asleep. They also use the sunlight to help make up for the slight drop in their body temperature once they're asleep.

Some cats even change their sleep positions to follow the movement of the sun.

Why does catnip 'flip out' your cat?

When your cat sniffs catnip, that wacky, daydreamy state she immediately enters is actually a response to the herb's powerful chemical, *trans-nepetalactone*. It's almost identical to the essence excreted by the female cat, which is why toms are said to love catnip the most. However, this doesn't explain why females love it.

Once, catnip was thought to be an aphrodisiac, but scientific tests squelched that theory. By the way, cats aren't attracted to it until they're at least two months old.

If you're out of catnip and Kitty's got a craving for the stuff, look in your spice rack: The herb valerian will give cats that same sense of ecstasy. Valerian is a mild stimulant and, though it doesn't do any harm, it shouldn't be offered to cats with kidney ailments.

Both catnip and valerian produce ecstasy through the odor, not the taste.

Why is a cat's tongue so raspy?

Depending on your own sensitivity, that little sandpaper tongue may delight or disturb you. To your cat, though, it's a vital tool.

Those little prickly things covering the upper surface of her tongue are called *papillae* and are actually a holdover from when her ancestors needed to keep a low profile in the wild. The tongue's upper surface has hundreds of small backward-pointing protuberances constructed of virtually the same substance as human fingernails. Your cat uses her tongue like a comb to give herself an extra-deep cleaning, so that she leaves no odor to warn her pray as she sneaks up on it.

Her tongue not only feels like a piece of sandpaper, it's even used like one – designed to scrape that last little bit of meat from bones. Of course, because of canned and packaged foods, this talent is no longer much needed by your average house cat, although the big African wild cats still use their tongues to pick the bones of carcasses clean, ensuring every last nutritious bite.

A newborn kitten has another special feature. At birth, the tongue has a rim of spines that runs along the edge. These spines help give the hungry kitten a good grip on Mom's nipple.

What's so special about a cat's teeth?

These guys are such wonderful rodent hunters, even their teeth are specially designed for mouse eating. Cats have 30 teeth, each specially adapted for a specific job – like stabbing, slicing and biting. The teeth are arranged so the cat can sever a rodent's spine with the precision of a surgeon. The large canine teeth let her grab her prey securely enough to kill it. Her molars work like scissors to cut prey into bite-size pieces.

Their mouths are also specially adapted for meat eating. They cannot move their jaws sideways like we humans do, so they are unable to grind or chew food with their mouths closed. That's why they always chew on large prey with the side of their mouth, cutting off large pieces and swallowing them whole.

Baby teeth – those tiny little protrusions that feel like needles – eventually get replaced by permanent ones. The replacement starts at about six months, and there is a full set of permanent teeth by nine months.

Why do cats drink dirty water?

It does seem unreasonable, doesn't it? There you go, washing her drinking bowl every day, then filling it with nice fresh tap water. What does she do? She ignores it and drinks from dirty puddles instead!

Your painstaking efforts may be just the reason she turns to the puddles. Why? Because of her keen sense of smell. Fresh tap water usually is heavily treated with chemicals and often chlorinated so strongly that it has a chemical odor – offending Kitty's sensitive nose. Even worse, you've probably washed her dish with some form of detergent. This doesn't usually interfere with her food bowls, since food odors disguise it. But add the unpleasant odor of tap water to the unpleasant odor of the water dish, and you've got a formula for failure. Stale water in puddles, aquariums and flower vases seems much more attractive to her. They're full of natural microbes and organic decomposing vegetation. To her, those flavors are divine.

If you're worried about her health, consider that most of the world's animals are doing just fine slurping naturally outdoors. But if you'd like to break yours of her habit, here's a hint: Be sure to wash all the detergent off her bowl, and let tap water stand for a while before offering it.

Why doesn't your cat like refrigerated food?

Considering how little they like cold food, it's odd that the sound of an opening refrigerator door brings them out of the woodwork so fast.

The reason they find cold food unappealing is because they're basically predators. In nature, they would consume their kills fresh – at body temperature. Try serving her food at room temperature, or giving it a quick zap in the microwave.

Are most cats left-'handed' or right-'handed'?

Paw-preference tests were conducted on 60 cats at Oxford University's physiology lab. Researchers found that the majority of the cats consistently used their left paw.

This led Dr. J. Cole of the university's lab to conclude that most cats are right-brain dominant. That's because the right-brain hemisphere controls movement on the left side of the body, and vice versa. Right-brain dominance also means your cat is highly intuitive.

Other experts believe cats are ambidextrous.

Why do cats always land on their feet?

The short answer is, they don't. Sure, they're the champs when it comes to landing safely – most of the time. But keep in mind that even if they land upright, they can sustain severe injuries from the impact.

Their amazing acrobatic skill is due to their natural 'righting' reflex. This mechanism is very complicated, and is governed by a complex organ in the inner ear that determines a specific sequence of events. Simplified, this organ sends information to the brain about the position of the cat's head in relation to the ground. In fractions of seconds, the brain commands the head to change position in order to protect it. When her head is level, she first flips the top half of her body around to face the ground, then flips the rear. In the process, she uses her tail to adjust for any overbalance. Finally, she's ready for landing, and reaches the ground on all four feet with her back arched to cushion the impact.

The trick to her success, though, is time. She needs a minimum of 1.8 seconds to 'right' herself. Though she is able to accomplish this in a fall as short as one-foot, her chances of success are much better at greater heights (within limits).

Experts say few cats would survive a fall of more than 60 feet, but it was 'no contest' when the *Guinness Book of Pet Records* heard about Gros Minou, a two-year-old ginger-and-white tomcat who fell 200 feet from his owner's 20th-floor balcony in Quebec, Canada. Gros Minou landed in a flower bed and sustained nothing more than a fractured pelvis. Within a week, he was crawling about.

However, a cat named Patricia actually beat Gros Minou's record by falling five feet further (205 feet) – and surviving; but since Patricia fell (or was thrown) from St. John's Bridge into the cold waters of the Willamet River, Gros Minou still holds the record for a *terra firma* tumble. I guess that's called a 'ground' rule.

How can cats jump so high?

Mother Nature gave her this skill to aid in her hunting abilities. Strong muscles in her hind quarters and back provide most of her jumping power. When she crouches, she tips back her pelvis and bends the three joints of her hip, knee and ankle. These joints have little or no sideways mobility and are designed to handle a strong impact down the entire length of her body.

When the muscles contract, these joints quickly extend, forcing her body forward. The strongest muscle runs along both sides of her spine and enables her to spring up in the air or leap huge distances.

Fortunately, she doesn't have to think much about this. This amazing creature can leap from a standing position to five times her height with hardly any effort.

How does a cat know how high to jump?

It has to do with her eyes.

Cats' faces are flat between the eyes, so both eyes are able to work together more easily. This is a rare feature in the animal world. But because of it, your kitty has an amazing ability to visually judge distances with remarkable accuracy. As a result, she can focus more sharply and actually see three-dimensionally.

Why are cats such finicky eaters?

Your cat likes to eat fresh food – a little bit at a time, yet quite often. Considering the size of the average mouse, small meals are the order of the day. A typical meal of commercial cat food, by the way, equals five mice.

Kitty also prefers to dine out of clean bowls and in a private, quiet place.

If her mealtime ritual is not perfect, your cat may turn up her nose at supper. Of course, if she's hungry enough, she'll eat almost anything (except fruit).

If your cat continually avoids food, there could be several reasons: If she's an outdoor cat, she might be getting her food elsewhere. She may be experiencing discomfort in her mouth or teeth (check to see if she's excessively pawing or rubbing her mouth and face – it may mean she has a toothache or bad gums). Stress or depression will affect her appetite. Leaving food out too long or serving it too cold also turn her off. If you keep her food in the fridge, try heating it slightly before serving.

Finally, food finickiness may even be built in to your cat. Cat behaviorist Desmond Morris notes they actually prefer lots of variety. This is nature's way of making sure they can always find a new food supply if the old supply dwindles. If they didn't have this ability, they would likely starve.

Studies have actually shown that when cats are given a choice between a routine food or a new food, they almost always choose the new variety.

What are some of the weirder things they eat?

What is it about these crazy cats that makes them snub their sensitive noses at fabulous food, then wash down the most awful stuff with fresh toilet water?

A sable Burmese from Minnesota loves to drink homemade tomato juice from the breakfast table; and I know a cat that eats artichokes!

But probably the most unusual appetite belonged to a cat owned by Mrs. Lorraine Ford. *Cat World* magazine in 1985 reported that her cat not only ate grapes, but would neatly spit the pits into a pile!

How can they eat so much garbage and not get sick?

Well, actually, sometimes, they do. After all, there are degrees of rotten food, even for a garbage picker. For the most part, though, cats are naturally safeguarded against food-related illness because they have specially designed gastric juices that protect them. These special chemicals not only can digest unchewed pieces of food but can also break down bones and destroy bacteria in the food.

This same cat also ate garlic cheese, chili con carne, pasta, baked beans, corn kernels, mashed potatoes, hard-boiled eggs, yogurt and honey, cakes and ice pops.

Despite their finickiness, an average cat consumes about 127,750 calories a year, nearly 28 times her own weight in food, and the same amount again in liquids.

In case you're wondering, no, cats *cannot* survive on a vegetarian diet.

Why do they eat plants?

Cats nibble plants indoors as a substitute for eating grass, which is perfectly natural behavior. Eating grass is like taking medication – it's nature's way of inducing vomiting.

The reason your cat needs to regurgitate (vomit) is to rid her digestive system of those painful hairballs that accumulate from her grooming. Because she can't very well stick a paw down her throat to do the job, she instinctively seeks out grasses or plants.

Since she'll eat almost anything green, it's important that she doesn't have access to plants that are toxic – like philodendron, dieffenbachia and English ivy, to name just a few. You can make sure that what she gnaws on is safe by buying special grasses sold at pet stores. She will also love parsley, sage, thyme and lavender.

Why do cats sleep so much?

They're downright cat-atonic, aren't they? Sleeping practically all day, every day – clocking in about 16 hours of dozing during every 24-hour period. That's almost twice the sleep we humans get!

Even how they sleep can be funny – from sitting up to snuggling into spots you'd never dream suitable (one of my furry friends curls himself into a pasta bowl!)

Certainly, these laid-back critters aren't exactly the labor force of the animal kingdom. So what's up with all that snoozing they do?

They're the cat-nap originators. Your kitty's sleep patterns have evolved because of her ancestors' success as a predator. Their bodies are designed for short bursts of energy needed for high-performance over short distances. They're so efficient at stalking and killing their prey that they end up with time to spare. What better way to relax than on a full stomach?

Also, they sleep very lightly, so they make up in the length of time they sleep what they lack in depth of sleep. And R&R has become part of their lifestyle.

Curiously, though, even in deep sleep, their brains are always on the alert for danger. So don't try pulling your tabby's tail when she's snoozing: She'll wake up in a split-second and may strike out at you in the process.

How well can a cat hear?

I'll bet *you* can't hear the refrigerator door opening in the kitchen . . . when you're upstairs . . . in the bedroom . . . under the covers . . . fast asleep. It's a pretty good bet, though, your feline companion can.

So how good is her hearing? Actually, dogs have a greater range of pitch, but your cat's hearing far exceeds a dog's when it comes to picking out high-pitched sounds. Cats, after all, have brilliantly adapted to hunting by lurking in bushes – listening for the tiniest sound, the smallest rustle, the tiniest squeak. Their keen hearing also lets them know the precise direction and distance of their victims. No mouse is safe.

They can hear sounds up to an amazing 100,000 cycles per second which – no coincidence here – happens to be about the same sound pitch made by a mouse's squeal. A cat's hearing capability is five times greater than humans.

(Dogs have only one-third the hearing ability of cats!) No wonder your screeching stereo drives the poor thing mad!

Author and cat-watcher Desmond Morris says their amazing sound sensitivity is the reason many people mistakenly believe that cats have extrasensory or supernatural powers. They can indeed hear ultrasonic sounds that precede a noisy activity such as an earthquake. They can wake up from a dead sleep before your spouse's car pulls into the driveway.

Given her amazing power of hearing, isn't it curious that Kitty appears entirely deaf to your orders?

So how *do* cats predict earthquakes and the weather?

For centuries, the Chinese have been looking to cats for early warning of earthquakes. Scientists monitoring earth tremors in California say cats can sense them long before the most delicate of instruments can.

We probably won't be replacing our high-tech instruments with cats anytime soon. But there's no doubt that cats do seem to flee just *before* earthquakes occur. There are several theories as to why.

One old wives' tale, for example, actually may have some basis in scientific fact. It says that a cat passing her paw over her ear signals an oncoming storm. The real reason could be that the cat is trying to massage away the annoying sensation of electrical waves that pass through the air when a storm is building. (I'll admit, this does get a bit technical, but read on – it's very inter-

49

esting!) Before a storm actually strikes, there's an enormous buildup of electricity and the air becomes highly charged with particles that are thought to influence brain chemistry. (Some of you may even get a headache before thunder.)

Naturalist Ivan Sanderson thinks cats' astonishing ability to high-tail it out of an area before a quake strikes is really a result of their *supersensory perception* – a highly sensitive way of hearing that lets them pick up annoying noises inside the earth.

Why are kittens born with their eyes closed?

All kittens are born blind, and their eyes remain closed as a protective measure until this delicate sense begins to develop. (They're also born deaf, incidentally.)

Since your kitty's perfect balance requires a combo of eye and ear messages, the tiny kitten's righting reflex isn't fully operational until her eyes open. Kittens will begin to open their eyes five to 10 days after they're born, and their eyes open fully between eight and 20 days.

Once their eyes are open, kittens then have to 'learn' how to handle all the visual stimuli coming through them, and are unlikely to master all these skills until they're approximately 12 weeks old.

Their sense of smell, though, is well developed from day one. Even at birth, certain behaviors are instinctive. If you hold your finger up to a newborn kitten's nose, for example, she'll hiss or spit if she feels disturbed.

At birth, all kittens' eyes are blue/gray; they get their permanent eye color at about 12 weeks.

How can you tell if a kitten is a boy or a girl?

Lots of luck! Believe me, you won't be the first to find out that your he-kitty is actually a she!

Humorist Sally Poplin had a cat called Ben Hur. She called it Ben, Poplin says – until the cat had kittens.

Actually, it's easiest to tell a kitten's sex when he/she is just a few hours old because the clues aren't all covered up by fur. But if you haven't got a front-row seat when Mom first brings her kitties into the world, forget it. You'll have to wait until they're 10 or 12 weeks old.

At that time, you can spot the differences this way: In females, the orifice is slit-like; in males, it's round. Also, the distance between the anus and the sexual opening is greater in males than in females.

How long will a cat nurse her young?

As a rule, kittens are fully weaned at eight weeks. But as early as three or four days after giving birth, Mom already will begin to leave the 'nest' for short periods.

For the first couple of days, though, her little brood will hang on almost continually to her teats, even when they stop drinking and fall asleep. It's crucial at this stage that the kittens each have a steady milk supply. From that special brew, they not only get lots of nutrition, they also get antibodies that help guard them against disease.

Although Momma has eight teats, if she gives birth to more than six kittens, they may not each get enough to eat. That's why it's critical that each newborn stakes out a special nipple of her own.

Nature has taken care of this problem in a remarkable way. Believe it or not, each one of Momma's nipples has its own special smell. Once the kitten assigns herself to that nip-

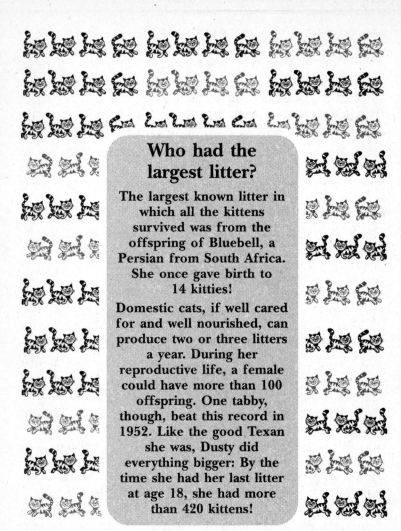

Who had the largest litter?

The largest known litter in which all the kittens survived was from the offspring of Bluebell, a Persian from South Africa. She once gave birth to 14 kitties!

Domestic cats, if well cared for and well nourished, can produce two or three litters a year. During her reproductive life, a female could have more than 100 offspring. One tabby, though, beat this record in 1952. Like the good Texan she was, Dusty did everything bigger: By the time she had her last litter at age 18, she had more than 420 kittens!

ple, she will always recognize it with ease. This helps to avoid potentially frantic and noisy scramblings for milk, and keeps feeding time a rather civilized – though piled-up – affair.

Why do most cats hate water?

Considering that cats evolved practically as desert animals, in climates that were very dry, it's not so surprising that they aren't nuts about water. There just wasn't a whole lot of it around!

In reality, though, virtually any cat who has been exposed to water since kittenhood may enjoy it – and might even delight in taking a bath once in a while.

The key word here is might! You won't know unless you try; but don't push it.

Certain breeds do seem to like water more than others; Abyssinians have even been known to join their owners in the shower. The Van cat, rare outside her native Turkey, loves to swim. Turkish angoras and Manxes also enjoy water.

A wild cat, known as 'the fishing cat' may be the most unique: This one actually swims to catch fish. Called the Bengali Mach-Bagral, nature gave her extra-long claws which she uses like fish hooks to spear them. This fishing cat is found in Nepal, Burma, Southern China and parts of India.

Should you bathe your cat?

If Kitty had anything to say about it, the answer definitely would be 'no'. They're not nuts about this water business in the first place, and probably feel downright insulted that you seem to think they can't handle the job of grooming themselves perfectly well on their own.

As a rule, only bathe a cat if she's very dirty or if she has a disease that requires bathing. If you absolutely must bathe her, use a gentle shampoo and always do it in a well-heated room, in a tub of lukewarm water (about 86 degrees Fahrenheit).

Be gentle and never scare her by running water on her or spraying her with it. Scoop the water over her, never wet her head, and always rub her dry with a prewarmed towel. Some cats don't object to a hair dryer; though mine can't even stand the sound of one.

How long can a cat go without food or water?

You won't have to drive yourself nuts worrying about a finicky cat who refuses to eat. She can survive without food much longer than we can. In fact, she can lose as much as 40 percent of her body weight and survive.

Not that you'd ever want to test this theory, but your pet can go without food for two or three days without even getting very hungry – and up to two weeks with no ill effects.

Water is another matter entirely. A 10 to 14 percent loss of the total water in your cat's body is fatal.

Of course, there are the exceptional cases: Chips, a marmalade tom from Liverpool, England, for example, was inadvertently packed into a crate of machine parts and shipped by sea to Mombasa. Four weeks later, when the crate was opened in Africa, Chips was still alive – though he looked like he'd been on Weight Watchers!

Why do they have so many babies?

Mother Nature was kind to cats when it came to guaranteeing the survival of the species. First of all, your cat can get pregnant as early as six months of age. Plus, the feline reproductive cycle is set up so that the female cat doesn't actually ovulate until she has been stimulated by a male cat. In other words, her eggs are released and available for fertilization only after the male's sperm has been introduced into her reproductive tract. Because she ovulates instantly when she mates, the odds that she will become pregnant are greatly increased.

Why do kittens in a litter all look so different?

Believe it or not, they probably all had different fathers!

One of the more bizarre biological attributes of a female cat is that she can go into heat while she's already pregnant. In fact, her ovaries are stimulated to release more eggs as soon as one male partner withdraws. So a single litter of kittens can have more than one father.

Mating isn't exactly a romantic affair – the whole process only takes a couple of seconds. Once a male cat has finished, the female will wait for another tom to approach her. Depending on the neighborhood, one roaming tom after another may mate with her. After that, it's anyone's guess whose sperm fertilized which egg. She can even carry two litters at the same time at two different stages of development!

How long do cats carry their litter?

The average gestation period of a cat is nine weeks, or 63 days.

One of the oddest things I recall about one cat's pregnancy was that, knowing she was 'with child', I began observing her carefully from day one. But there was hardly an external sign to be seen; then suddenly – on about the 35th day – she expanded like a balloon.

If you're not sure just when your cat got pregnant, you

can figure out her due date by noticing when her nipples first begin to redden. This is known as 'pinking up' and occurs approximately during the third week of pregnancy. You can do the arithmetic from there.

Kittens which are born earlier than 58 days tend to be born very weak or, worse, dead. Kittens born very late, after 71 days for instance, also are likely to be born dead. Consult your veterinarian if she's carrying this long; she may need your help.

Some females have been known to continue to breed well into their senior years – as old as age 12 (and there have been some even older than that).

Why are kittens born with their ears folded?

Answering this question takes a bit of glancing backward: Let's start way back at the beginning – at the time of pregnancy. As we've said, cats have a relatively short gestation period. One of the reasons nature has made it so brief is so that cats can get pregnant more often and have more babies.

But having so many babies often means kittens don't get a chance to fully develop all their senses before coming into the world. Eyesight and hearing – two of the most complicated – take time to properly mature.

So the kitten actually is born deaf. The ear canal is closed and not fully developed. Nature, however, gives the kittens sort of a 'breather' by allowing their ears to continue developing after they are born. The little tyke's ears are sort of folded to protect the internal mechanism until development is complete.

It takes about 14 days for the ear canal to open up. Until then, Kitty relies on signals she can actually feel, such as the vibrations of her Mom's purring.

Why do they walk the way they do?

Even the way your cat walks suits her as a skillful hunter.

Almost all animals walk by moving alternate legs: first the left front and right rear; then the right front and left rear.

Only three animals walk by moving the two legs on one side together first, and then shifting to do the same on the other side: the giraffe, the camel and, you guessed it, your cat.

This method of walking – which is basically diagonal – uses a minimum amount of energy and helps ensure speed, agility and silence.

Why do cats spend so much time grooming?

The typical cat devotes about a third of her waking day grooming herself. Considering how many hours she devotes to sleep, this may not sound like much – but it translates to about three hours' worth of self-pampering a day. How many of us can afford to indulge in such luxury!

There are several reason she grooms herself so fastidiously. Cats clean themselves with their saliva, which is thought to contain a detergent-like deodorizing substance that keeps her coat soft, glossy and clean. But grooming also has other important functions: It removes dead hair and skin, tones up her muscles and stimulates blood circulation (this is also why Momma cat cleans her newborns so frequently.)

How do cats use their whiskers?

How their whiskers work isn't fully understood (except by your cat, of course), but there's no doubt they are one of her most sensitive features. By bending her whiskers like antennae, your cat can magnify the smallest air disturbances. With these fabulous feelers, she can safely maneuver through underbrush and around obstacles, and avoid bumping into things.

Kitty's whiskers – called *vibrissae* – grow at the side of her mouth in four rows and above her eyes. There are approximately 25 to 30 of them, each attached to a nerve in the skin. They are so sensitive, your cat can rely on them to aid her movement in the dark. She actually can 'identify' things she can't see. Studies of blindfolded cats, for example, reveal they can place their front paws on a table top when only their whiskers had touched its edge.

The slightest touch on a whisker also causes a reflex closing of the eye. This is especially vital protection for your feline hunter whose eyes are frequently fixed on prey. It also ensures that a twig or grass springing back doesn't cause injury.

Whiskers are so important to your cat that removal of them actually can harm her. Some scientists theorize that Kitty bends some or all of her whiskers downward to help guide her when jumping or leaping over uneven ground.

A cat with poor eyesight will use her whiskers like a blind person uses a cane. Kitty will walk with her head moving from side to side, using her whiskers to guide her.

So it's no surprise then, that when something is really wonderful we say it's the cat's whiskers.

How can a cat crawl through an opening smaller than her body?

This ability is due to her remarkable collarbone. Or more precisely – its absence.

She has little or no collarbone at all, and her chest cavity is small for her size. Together, this makes her practically collapsible.

Graceful creature that she is, she'll always think through a situation before plunging in. You can watch her carefully figure out the height or width of an opening before she actually attempts to invade it. She does this with the help of her whiskers.

If a cat lost her tail, would it affect her sense of balance?

Maybe this is a good time for a joke: If your cat loses her tail, where can she get a new one? Answer: In a re-tail store, of course!

Actually, a lost tail is no laughing matter. It obviously was put there for a reason. Your cat uses her tail for balance very much like a tightrope walker uses a long pole. If she's walking along a narrow wall or a fence and decides to peer over in one direction, she automatically moves her tail in the other direction.

However, cats can get along quite well with only the stub of a tail – or even no tail at all – if, say, they lose it in an accident.

Cats seem to be terrific compensators. If they weren't, there'd be no Manxes left by now.

How can cats walk in the snow and not get frozen paws?

Even though their footpads feel soft and smooth to you, they're actually very calloused areas. The pads are made of a modified type of skin that covers a thick cushion of connective tissue, making them much tougher than normal skin. Because these areas are thicker, they offer some protection against the cold. And, of course, where there's no calloused skin, there's fur.

Why don't cats drink a lot of water?

Originally, your cat's ancestors were desert animals (that's why they still bury their litter in the sand, by the way).

Because of this, their kidneys have adapted incredibly well to life without water. As a result, their kidneys can eliminate a lot of harmful toxins into the urine without needing a lot of fluid to do so. That's why their urine is so concentrated – and also why it smells so awful.

Generally, the average healthy cat needs very little fluid to maintain her health. Research has shown that cats fed a steady diet of canned cat food – which is 70 percent water – may choose not to drink additional water. She may be getting all the fluid she needs with her food.

Nevertheless, fresh water should always be available.

Can a cat get a sunburn?

Not only can your cat get a sunburn, she even can wind up with a serious form of skin cancer as a result of too much sun.

White cats – with their little pink noses – are especially susceptible to something called *solar dermatitis*. The disease first appears around the nose and tips of the ears. If not treated, it can induce *squamous-cell carcinoma*, a dangerous form of cancer.

There are some remedies, though, that can help prevent Kitty from getting skin cancer. You can try using sunblock on those tender spots, but your cat isn't likely to like it much and, besides, she'll probably lick it all off before it has much effect.

Veterinarian James Grubb suggests a more permanent protective solution: tattooing. Using standard tattoo ink and the traditional needle-applied procedure, a vet will tattoo a line along the tips of the cat's ears, and on the cat's entire nose. Presumably, this gives the ultimate protection; but I wonder how you get "I Love Mom" to fit on that tiny nose?

What's the average length of a cat's life?

Never long enough.

But thankfully, the average life expectancy of a cat has increased tremendously, nearly doubling since 1930. You can expect Kitty to purr by your side from anywhere between eight to 16 years – that is, if she's lucky enough to spend her life in your loving home. The poor defenseless creatures who are fated to fend for themselves in the streets live only about three or four years. And those years are not very happy ones.

There are, of course, countless examples of cats who live to be really ripe old ages.

Who was the oldest cat?

The all-time senior-citizen cat record is still held by Puss, a cat who lived with Mrs. T. Holway of Devon, England, until she died on November 29, 1939 – just one day after her 36th birthday.

Soul & Personality

There is indeed no single quality of the cat that man
could not emulate to his advantage...

Carl van Vechten

Would she miss you if you went away?

Don't take this personally, but the answer probably is 'no'.

The truth is, cats really are more attached to a place than to a person. Remember, to your cat, you are simply an overgrown litter-mate. As long as she's left undisturbed and can go about her business in her familiar, comfortable home, it's likely that she's indifferent to whoever else is there with her. Provided, of course, that *someone* is there – after all, there are still those cans of food to pry open!

Having said that, it's been my experience that whenever I've been away for extended periods of time, my cats kill me with kindness when I return.

There's not a lot of scientific data that says that cats miss their owner – certainly not in the way dogs do. But there is definitely some bonding going on. When my TC was so ill that she was hospitalized for weeks, we visited her every day. The vet said she could practically measure TC's physical improvement immediately after our daily visit.

Can a lost cat find her way home?

Indeed she can. And the list of incredible Lost-Cat-Returns-Home stories is as long as some of the journeys themselves.

Like the one about a yellow tomcat belonging to an Army sergeant. When the sergeant was transferred from Kokomo, Indiana, to Augusta, Georgia – a distance of 700 miles – he took the kitty with him. The cat made that trip in a closed box on an express train, so there was no possible way she ever could have known the route. Well, imagine how surprised the sergeant was when his kitty disappeared and showed up back in Indiana – in less than three weeks!

How did she do that?

A cat's uncanny ability to travel enormous distances over totally unknown territory to return to their homes is called *psi trailing*. For decades, it's been under serious study by Duke University's parapsychology laboratory. Still, no one quite understands exactly how cats do this.

Psi trailing certainly demonstrates a cat's amazing physical (perhaps even supernatural, some say) ability – not to mention her loyalty, devotion and love. But many experts laugh at the weird theories, and suggest instead that the true answer is not so bizarre.

Your cat's amazing homing ability may rely on a built-in navigation system similar to that used by birds. She subconsciously registers the angle of the sun at certain times of day.

When she's taken away from home, she finds her way back again by using a combination of her internal biological clocks, trial and error and the angle of the sun. She's so good at doing this that she doesn't even need a clear day to navigate – she's that sensitive to the earth's magnetic fields.

Regardless, let's say the cat doesn't use supernatural power, but actually manages to find her way back home over several hundred unknown miles based on this complicated scientific formula. I think that's still pretty amazing. Don't you?

What was the longest distance a cat traveled using psi trailing?

An unbelievable 1,500 miles – clocked by a cream-colored semi-Persian named Sugar. In addition to her pretty, cream-colored coat, Sugar had a distinctively deformed bone in her left hip.

When Sugar's family moved from California to Oklahoma, they didn't take the kitty because she was terrified of cars. So the Smiths left Sugar in the care of a kindly neighbor. One afternoon, after the Smiths had been in their new Oklahoma home about a year, a cat who looked exactly like Sugar suddenly appeared and leaped onto Mrs. Smith's shoulder as she was kneeling in the garden.

The cat even had Sugar's same hip deformity.

When they investigated, they learned that, sure enough, Sugar had disappeared weeks earlier from her adoptive home – and had tracked her family over desert, mountains and highways more than 1,500 miles!

There was never a mention, however, of what condition her cream-colored coat was in when she got there!

Do cats have a sixth sense?

Sort of. A cat's sixth sense is actually something midway between taste and smell. Her receptor is called the Jacobson's organ and is located in the roof of the cat's mouth. It is thought to communicate signals to the sexual center of the cat's brain.

When the Jacobson's organ is stimulated, the cat opens her mouth slightly and wrinkles her nose – a response called the 'flehmen reaction'. The curious grimace occurs when some particularly stimulating odors are detected. This behavior was first described and named by a former director of the Leipzig Zoo in Germany, Dr. Karl-Marx Schneider. For lack of an appropriate English word, the term *flehmen* (pronounced flay-men) is used.

Do cats have ESP?

Well, yes...and no.

Experimental psychologist, David Greene, has spent years studying the mind of the cat and firmly believes any cat can perform amazing extrasensory feats.

Behaviorist Desmond Morris, however, ignores the ESP theory altogether. He maintains that anything we perceive as coming through our senses is not *extra*-sensory. In fact, Morris suggests that the actual scientific or biological explanations of some of our cats' most remarkable behaviors is even more fascinating than simply explaining them away as magic – their ultra-sensitivity to sound, for instance, when people are approaching; their acute sensitivity to changes in static electricity that causes them to anticipate earthquakes; and their indisputable homing ability.

Can astrology apply to cats?

In Chinese astrology, every 12th year is called the Year of the Cat, and is supposed to mean happy times are coming. The Chinese believe that people born in a cat year are decent, clever and have a high regard for others. Even more to the cat-like point, those people are assumed to be a bit aloof and oversensitive. Perhaps your birthday is among these previous Years of the Cat (also known as the Year of the Rabbit): 1927, 1939, 1951, 1963, 1975, 1987. The next one is 1999.

What can astrology tell you about your cat?

According to author Michael Zullo, plenty. Zullo compiled *Cat Astrology* (Tribune Publishing, Orlando, 1993), which lists personality characteristics to help give you a 'paw up', so to speak, in understanding your cat.

Considering how many cats just show up in our lives one day, it isn't always possible to know your cat's precise birthday. But it may be worth perusing these traits to see if you can figure it out – in reverse.

See if you can find your cat among these:

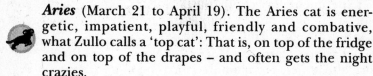

Aries (March 21 to April 19). The Aries cat is energetic, impatient, playful, friendly and combative, what Zullo calls a 'top cat': That is, on top of the fridge and on top of the drapes – and often gets the night crazies.

Taurus (April 20 to May 20). The Taurus cat is routine-minded, home-loving, stubborn, predictable, calm (unless provoked, that is). The Taurus cat will get along with everyone, unless her personal schedule is disrupted.

Gemini (May 21 to June 21). The Gemini cat is spirited, mischievous, fun-loving, attention-getting and clever. She's so energetic, it's like owning two cats in one.

Cancer (June 22 to July 22). The Cancer cat is affectionate, devoted, moody, sensitive and nurturing – the purrfect cat for your lap.

Leo (July 23 to August 22). The Leo cat is proud, self-centered, showy, cunning and loves attention. Consider your Leo cat King of the house, because she does.

Virgo (August 23 to September 22). The Virgo cat is cautious, fussy, shy and prefers her own company. She hates surprises and would have been a CPA if she weren't a cat.

Libra (September 23 to October 23). The Libra cat is happy, vocal, sociable, indecisive and well-behaved. Very friendly and outgoing, it's hard to remember she's a cat and not a person.

Scorpio (October 24 to November 21). The Scorpio cat is demanding, territorial, strong-willed and fierce. This cat sees the world on her own terms and has the nerve and guts to do what she wants, whenever she wants.

Sagittarius (November 22 to December 21). The Sagittarius cat is playful, daring, curious and messy. She is a naturally happy cat, for whom the world is a toy – including you.

Capricorn (December 22 to January 19). The Capricorn cat is crafty, persistent, reserved, moody and possessive. Defining her is a little tricky. Generally, though, your Capricorn cat will always be there for you. She's cautious, persistent but not stubborn; and loves snuggling under the covers.

Aquarius (January 20 to February 18). The Aquarius cat is unpredictable, frisky, curious, an attention grabber and sociable. This is definitely a cat of action with psychic abilities that enable her to foresee things before they happen.

Pisces (February 19 to March 20). The Pisces cat is quiet, easygoing, sweet and devoted. Nothing is a big deal to her – except sleep. She sleeps more than any other cat.

Which cat had the most amazing misadventure?

Certainly Jacob's story ranks as one of the most amazing. One coal-black night in the winter of 1964, a Dutch ship called the *Tjoba*, moved cautiously down the River Rhine. Suddenly, an unexpected and violent collision left the boat so damaged that it immediately started to sink and, within minutes, was on the river bottom.

All the crewmen were saved; but sadly, Jacob, the ship's six-year-old cat, was trapped below deck and went down with the vessel.

Eight days later, when cranes had raised the wreck, the crew went aboard to collect whatever was left of their waterlogged belongings. Was the captain ever surprised when he opened his cabin door. The last thing he ever expected to see was Jacob. But there he was, shivering with cold and hunger. To everyone's utter amazement, Jacob had survived more than a week underwater – in a bubble of trapped air!

Do cats really want to die alone?

This is a myth that just won't die.

For ages, we've romanticized the notion that cats have a need to die alone – in the wild, joined with the earth, without the intrusion of their human friends.

The truth is, cats haven't the foggiest notion about death; so they can hardly plan for what they don't know. What they do know, however, is whether or not they are being threatened by illness or injury. In either case, it's as if they're being chased by a predator they cannot see. Understandably, their instinct simply tells them to hide where the predator can't find them.

Sadly, what they don't know is that they take this 'predator' with them no matter where they hide. As a result, they may die alone without the help they need or the comfort they deserve – even from those who love them most.

Do tomcats really kill their kittens?

Tomcats are getting a bad rap on this point. They are not regular kitten-killers.

This notion may have come about quite literally 'by accident'. Toms have been known to actively participate in the rearing of their young. They do this, it is thought, so that the female will detach herself from her kittens and focus on going back into heat for him.

In the process, the sexually-aroused toms kill kittens accidentally: In the heat of passion, they may mount a female kitten, accidentally killing her with the ritualistic neck bite associated with mating.

On the other hand, two of my own male cats – Val and Tom – actually behaved as surrogate Moms. While they couldn't exactly provide nursing services, of course, they did express the gentlest and tenderest instincts around Pepper's newborn kittens. It was quite a heartwarming sight to behold.

Did black cats always represent bad luck?

Nope. Even during medieval days – that darkest period in cat history – a few cats were spared. The black cat was universally believed to be the dreaded 'devil cat'; but if one happened to cross your path without anything horrible happening, she was suddenly considered good luck!

King Charles I of England was convinced his black cat brought him good luck – and he carried his pet with him everywhere. When the cat died, Charles was disturbed and feared his life would never be the same. He reportedly said that his luck was gone. Boy, was he right: The next day, he was arrested and later beheaded.

Don't some cats routinely kill their young?

No cat kills her young as a matter of course. During a difficult delivery – if a kitten is stuck, for instance – she may accidentally mutilate or eat her in an attempt to pull it out.

There is some evidence that felines may have once had an instinct for cannibalism. Some observers even suggest that cannibalism is linked to a shortage of certain hormones, and that she ate kittens to make up for this deficiency. There is no scientific evidence to support this, however.

Will a nursing cat accept an adopted kitten?

Absolutely. Nursing cats actually are terrific adoptive parents. Of course, you can help encourage her along by smearing a bit of butter onto the tiny orphan. In the process of licking the butter from the kitten, she'll become the new Momma!

Nursing cats even have been known to lovingly rear orphans of another species, like squirrels, pigs and even timber wolf cubs. What's really bizarre, though, is that they've sometimes raised orphaned litters of rats or mice. However, they think nothing of hunting those rodents' family in the wild!

Is a cat a serious threat to a bird?

It's certainly true that, given half a chance, any self-respecting cat will find the temptation of a fluttering bird just too good an opportunity to pass up. And if your kitty roams outdoors, you've surely seen one bird too many caught in her jaws.

Many experts, however, suggest that cats do not present

71

a serious threat at all to birds. In reality, the unfortunate decreases in the bird population around the world is more likely the result of the destruction of their habitats due to poisons in the food chain and pollution. Most cats, in fact, very rarely succeed in catching healthy adult birds...and even then, it's only if their luck is good. To a cat, chasing birds – not necessarily catching one – is more like joining a gym. It simply keeps them in shape.

Why do some people fear a cat will suffocate a newborn baby?

This is a superstition that probably dates back to medieval times when cats were considered to be evil spirits. In those days, it was believed cats could suck the breath from sleeping infants.

This myth persisted even into our own time: "There were people who said it was dangerous to leave a cat with a baby," wrote Ernest Hemingway in *A Moveable Feast.* "The most ignorant and prejudiced said that a cat would suck a baby's breath and kill him." Hemingway, a notorious cat-lover who completely rejected the notion, was even criticized in the 1920s for allowing his cat, F. Puss, to sleep alongside his own small son.

Even though a cat would never deliberately harm an infant, it's never a good idea to leave any animal alone with an unwatched baby. To the animal, all those warm blankets that baby is bundled up in are an open invitation to snuggle up inside the crib. In this manner, a mature cat – who probably weighs more than the infant – might accidentally harm a newborn.

Why were cats worshiped
in ancient Egypt?

As we know, the ancient Egyptians were the first to keep cats in their homes. But even earlier, they held all cats in very high regard. Lions were trained and kept by Egyptian kings as symbols of power and, of course, as a practical means of defense against enemies.

Egyptians also viewed felines as awe-inspiring and mysterious. They thought a cat's eyes could protect them from evil. Their glow-in-the-dark eyes were thought to mirror the sun; so cats were believed capable of saving the world from eternal darkness. Egyptian women even imitated the beauty of cats' eyes by outlining their own in black. The cat's habit of sleeping curled up with her head touching her tail came to symbolize eternity. Cat funerals, in fact, were so elaborate in Egypt that kitties were buried in their own tiny coffins with mice mummies included to provide a tasty afterworld snack.

By 950 B.C., the foremost female Egyptian deity was Bastet, goddess of fertility and love, who took feline form. Domestic cats were thought to be her earth-bound representatives, and killing a cat (except in an official sacrifice to Bastet) was considered a crime punishable by death.

Why do cats play?

Because it's fun. Wouldn't you be pretty active, too, if you could shimmy up a drape like Spider Man?

All that playful rough-and-tumble stuff comes naturally to your feline acrobat. It's Nature's way of guaranteeing that she'll have all the skills she'll need for survival – therefore, she swats your shoe instead of a bird; and bats a ball of yarn instead of scooping up fish from a stream.

Playtime with her kitty brothers and sisters is also very important. It helps to tone her muscles and helps her develop her remarkable reflexes.

Very quickly, though, your kitten's never-ending play will begin to slow down – at about the age of five months. Experts think the reason for this decline in their frolicking is because nature assumes Kitty would already be out on her own, making her way as a hunter – if she were born in the wild. Yours of course, was not. But time ticks on anyway.

Even so, it should comfort you to know that domestic cats can play well into old age. They just won't be climbing the drapes anymore.

Why are cats such fierce fish-lovers?

It's an interesting question, considering that because of a cats' desert origins, they probably never even saw a fish.

Eighteenth-century naturalist Gilbert White thought their love for fish went against nature. He wrote about this subject in *A Natural History of Selbourne*: They have a "...violent fondness of fish which appears to be their most favorite food; yet nature seems to have planted in them an appetite that, unassisted, they know not how to gratify."

Enter the human factor.

Indeed, it's very likely that we humans are responsible for introducing them in the first place. Even today, except for snatching the odd goldfish from an unguarded fish tank now and then, it's still rare that a cat will hunt for fish in the wild. (However, there is one fish-hunting feline that lives in India.)

The cats' permanent connection with fish seems to have started during World War II. At that time, when most foods were hard to come by and carefully rationed, fish was an easily acquired and relatively cheap source of protein. Pet food manufacturers decided it would be a great substitute for expensive and hard-to-get meat.

No matter how much Kitty loves fish, she must eat meat for good nutrition and total health: She's a carnivore, after all.

74

History & Folklore

To err is human. To purr feline.
Author Robert Byrne

Where did the word 'cat' come from?

The word 'cat' seems strikingly similar in almost all European languages: in French, it's *chat*; in German, *katze*; Italian, *gatto*; Spanish *gato*; in Swedish, *katt*; and in Polish, *kot*. The original source, however, may be Arabic – where the word is *quttah* – since all domestic cats originally descended from the North African wild cat courtesy of the Egyptian domestication.

The ancient Egyptians called their domestic cats *miaw* and adorned them with jewels and gold earrings. The word *cat* first came into popular use during the fourth century and could have originally derived from the Nubian word *kadis*. It is likely that the word was then passed on – along with the cat herself – throughout the great Mediterranean and European trade routes.

Where did tabbies get their name?

The term 'tabby' actually comes from the Spanish word *tabi*, which was used to describe a popular and sought-after watered-silk cloth from the East. Your cat's mottled fur – with her stripes and bar markings – resembles the markings of that tabi-cloth and so came to be called tabby.

Where did the first cat come from?

Scientists theorize that the first feline ancestor was the *Miacis* – a creature described as an evil-tempered, weasel-like, meat-eating grouch. Certainly not the Kitty you know and love!

The Miacis was long-bodied and short-legged and roamed the earth about 40 million years ago.

An even more cat-like animal evolved from the Miacis in a mere one million years (a blink of an eye, by evolutionary standards). The *Ditictis*, as it was called, flourished during prehistoric times and was the ancestor of the 35 feline species that exist today.

The African wildcat (*Felis libya*) is thought to be the closest relative of your domestic Kitty. He looks a whole lot like your little one, only bigger.

How did cats first get to America?

The ancestors of today's American cats sailed to the New World during the early 1600s (despite the widespread superstition that they caused shipwrecks.) The first domestic cats to reach our shores were a pair of ratters given as a gift from a French missionary to a Huron Indian chief. The chief had no idea what to do with these kitties, so he ignored them. They died without producing kittens. It wasn't until 1749 that cats actually were imported from England specifically to control – what else? – the rat population.

As a matter of fact, cats have even been officially credited with helping in the colonization of America. Honest.

An *Encyclopedia Americana* published a half-century ago says, "A great deal of the advance of agriculture as well as the spreading out over the vast woodland and prairies has been made possible by the domestic cat." Early pioneers had to deal with over 40 major types of rodents. Imagine: If there weren't all those cats performing their mouse-eating miracles, there might never have been enough food crops for the pioneers to survive. And, who knows? Maybe not even a good old U.S. of A today!

When did they first become house pets?

The first kitties to regularly hang out with humans probably came of their own free will – attracted by the bumper-crop of mice and rats that infested the grain storehouses of early Egyptian civilization. We know this from the carved or painted images of cats that were found on ancient Egyptian tomb walls. The scenes clearly showed that cats eventually came to share the Egyptians' homes.

But that was only 5,000 years ago, a mere blink of the eye when you think about it. Dogs, for instance, have been human sidekicks for more than 10,000 years – one reason why they're far more well-behaved! Cats, on the other hand, practically still have one paw in the jungle. It makes you wonder if they really are domesticated.

Okay, so are they domesticated?

Sort of. It's hard to say why some of Kitty's ancestors became domesticated in the first place. Desmond Morris suggests that there may have been a genetic change that altered the wild cats' behavior. For example, there might have been a quirky gene that eventually turned aggressive wildcats into the kitten-like creatures we know today. This may have been the first step toward domestication. Once these less-aggressive cats began associating with people, they may have grown smaller in size, too. So, technically speaking, cats still are only in the early stages of becoming a domestic animal.

This is not news to your cat.

Of course, she doesn't roar anymore. But many traits that characterize wild cats – such as her hunting instinct – still remain very strong in your kitty.

What is the origin of the 'cat's cradle'?

This string game – in which two players wind loops of strings back and forth between them – winds up making a cradle-like form that's just the right size for a cat.

In his book *Catlore*, Desmond Morris offers two explanations for the cat's connection to cradles and strings:

Eastern European custom believed that cats could increase a couple's fertility (probably because cats have so many litters). After a wedding, a ceremony was performed in which a cat was placed in a cradle that was then carried into the newlywed couple's house. The cradle – cat and all – was rocked back and forth in their presence. The ritual was an attempt to ensure an early pregnancy for the young bride.

Another explanation says that games similar to our string game are played by Eskimos and Congo tribesmen. Their games, though, have a magical significance. The act of constantly shifting the patterns of the string is believed to influence the path of the sun. In the stiflingly hot Congo, for example, the game is played to encourage the sun to rest; in the frigid North, it's to trap the sun in order to shorten the winter. In both cultures, the sun is believed to be a 'solar cat' symbolically caught in the string patterns.

Why were cats associated with witchcraft?

It was bound to happen. Cats were never mentioned in the Bible (except once in the Catholic version), and have long been viewed with suspicion by the early Christian church.

They probably were first associated with pagan religions. In the 13th century, the first witchcraft trials were held; and, perhaps because cats are such mysterious animals, very superstitious people believed that witches could turn into cats. Black cats in particular were thought to be the devil in disguise.

Cats didn't have a chance, and they were blamed for everything: from souring beer to spreading disease. It was commonly believed that their teeth contained venom, their flesh was poisonous, and their breath could cause disease and infection.

The cat's habit of prowling around at night further connected her to the devil and witchcraft. Any cat who was in the company of an old woman was assumed to be a witch's evil associate. More likely, poor kitties were just lost souls, befriended by women who were childless and lonely. And both suffered the cruelest fates for their friendship.

All this fear and hate eventually made them the target of

persecution. Hundreds of unfortunate cats were burned alive by people who believed they did the work of the devil.

By the 17th century, however, Kitty's remarkable ability to catch and destroy rats caused her to gain respect once again. Cats virtually rescued Europe from the ravages of the Great Plague.

The rest is history.

Do superstitions about cats still persist?

You bet! Even today, actors believe that yelling at a cat brings bad luck to a performance. And, while actors don't mind if a cat roams around the theater, they dread the thought of her ever crossing the stage. If a cat walks on stage, it is said to bring misfortune to the entire cast.

There are those who believe you can harness the soul and spirit of a cat. Claire Nahmad's *Cat Spells* features a collection of spells that bring luck, health and love.

Simply dreaming of a cat is said to have a magical meaning. If you dream of a black cat, for instance, you'll be lucky in anything you do; if you dream of a tortoise-shell cat, you'll be lucky in love; dreaming of a ginger cat indicates luck in money and business.

Dream of a black-and-white cat and you'll have luck with children; a tabby means luck with your home. Dreaming of a multicolored cat means luck making friends.

It's still widely believed that a cat leaving a sick man's house and refusing to return is an omen of the man's death. Winston Churchill's cat, a ginger tom, his longtime and devoted pet, suddenly left his bedside shortly before Churchill died.

Maybe these aren't superstitions after all?

Did cats ever play a role in war?

Did they ever! . . . and practically since the beginning of history.

When the ancient Persians were warring with the Egyptians, they hit on a strategy that defeated Egypt. At the time, of course, Egyptians were well-known cat worshipers. So the Persians strapped cats to their shields when they stormed an Egyptian fortress. The Egyptians could not offend their all-powerful cat goddess, Bastet, and so were forced to lay down their arms.

Years later, during World War II, a British officer in Burma did something similar: He thought up a clever way to get the Burmese to support the Allies against the Japanese. The officer knew that the Burmese considered the cat sacred, so he painted cat images on his army vehicles and kept white cats on the Army base. When the Burmese saw this, they believed the cat's sacred spirit must be with the British and quickly switched to 'the side of the angels'.

Real cats have played important roles, too; though some kitty lives may have been lost in the process. During World War I, 500,000 cats were used by the British army to give soldiers early warnings of gas attacks.

How did the cat-o'-nine-tails get its name?

How curious that this instrument of punishment actually has its roots in the same place where cat worship began. This painful whip was invented in ancient Egypt, and was made from the skins of sacred cats. A flogging with the cat-o'-nine-tails was actually intended to help unfortunate wrong-doers. It was said that during the painful lashings, the strength and intelligence of the cat were transferred to the person being punished.

In those days, though, the whip wasn't actually called 'cat-o'-nine tails'. More likely, this name came later when a similar whip was used to discipline seamen; but it wasn't made of cats' tails. When sailors in the early British fleets were punished, their lashes were delivered with a nine-strop whip that left marks on a sailor's back that resembled the scratches from a cat attack. So the whip commonly came to be called cat-o'-nine-tails.

The use of this whip even generated another common phrase: Sailors couldn't be lashed indoors on a ship, because there wasn't enough room to swing the whip. So sailors would be lashed up on the main deck. Today, we still describe a tiny place by saying, "There isn't room to swing a cat in here."

Why are so many cats named Kitty?

Maybe we cat owners just aren't creative enough to think up a more interesting name.

Actually, the reason is quite simple and has more to do with how cats have responded over the centuries to the names we keep giving them. There's a better chance your cat will respond more readily to her name if it ends with an 'ee' sound. So that's just what most of us have wound up doing. It's a way of keeping us from being ignored when we call our royal princesses in from the street.

So, the next time you're picking a name for your cat – and feel inclined to name her Duchess Letitia von Scissorpaws St. Cloud Tugger Bear – consider nicknaming her Kitty.

Frankly, she probably won't come until she's ready to anyway – no matter what name you call her.

Where did the nine lives theory come from?

Cats and the nine lives theory is well-known around the world. And while it's obviously impossible to have that many lives, cats do seem to fiercely cling on to the one life they've been given.

This nine lives thing may have come about as a result of people noticing how often cats manage to have all sorts of accidents and still come out smiling (even when limping)!

Nine has always been a mystical number (like the Trinity of Trinities, the luckiest of numbers); and it's possible that the aura of mystery and magic that has always surrounded cats led to this theory.

Just consider the cat's righting reflex (more about this amazing feat on page 42), and imagine how weird that might have seemed to a cat owner in the Middle Ages – who had no clue to the cat's biology. They definitely would have thought it was supernatural!

Where does 'catgut' come from?

You'll be relieved to know it doesn't come from cats! Except for the name, it has nothing to do with cats at all.

Catgut is a tough cord made from the organs of certain animals – sheep, hogs and horses mostly – but (whew!) not cats. It's used mainly for making surgical sutures (what doctors use to sew us up) and for strings of tennis rackets, archery bows and musical instruments.

If you want the gory details, the intestines of the donor animals are first cleaned, scraped and cured with an alkaline solution. They're then dried and polished before being woven into cords.

How it first got to be called catgut may have happened this way: These cords were first used for stringed musical instruments centuries ago. People at that time were familiar with the horrifying sounds of a cat in pain. The dreadful sounds produced by inexperienced musicians sounded just like the shrieks of these unfortunate kitties.

Today, with the invention of plastic, there's very little need for animal's intestines to be used for such products.

What's the connection between cats and the weather?

Folks have long believed that cats have an uncanny ability to predict the weather – particularly nasty weather, such as earthquakes, tornadoes and volcanic eruptions.

In Scotland and Japan, tortoise-shell cats were believed to be able to predict storms. In England, cats were thought to be able to predict floods. And when a cat jumped up onto a shelf or beam, country folk swore that high water was on the way.

In the Ozarks, if a cat lies curled up with her head and stomach facing upward, it's thought to indicate bad weather; but if she yawns and stretches, good weather is on the way.

In many eastern European countries, it was believed that evil spirits took possession of cats during thunderstorms – and that lightning bolts were the angels' way of driving the evil out of these cats. Because of this, many poor cats found themselves tossed out of doors during storms to guarantee that their owners' houses wouldn't be struck in the process.

Why do we say "it's raining cats and dogs?"

Here's what Desmond Morris had to say in his book *Cat-watching:* It seems that some folks a few centuries back weren't terribly bright, and made a really weird connection between cats and rain.

Most towns and cities in those days had really narrow and dirty streets, and some of the worst sewer systems you could imagine. Drainage was so awful that, during very heavy rainstorms, there would be major flooding.

There also were a lot of stray cats and dogs living on the streets in these towns. Without shelter, many of them very likely drowned during the flooding. When the rains ended, and townsfolk came back out into the streets, there were all these dead animals lying there.

"Where did they suddenly come from?" the townspeople wondered. And someone said, "Why, it must've rained cats and dogs!" Well, although it sounds pretty unbelievable, that's the story.

A more likely explanation is suggested by students of language: The Greek word for a waterfall is *catadupa*. If some classical Greek compared a heavy rainfall to a waterfall, he might have said "raining catadupa," and the phrase may eventually have evolved into 'it's raining cats and dogs'.

Who's the richest cat?

The most 'fortune-ate' cats were Hellcat and Brownie. According to the *Guinness Book of World Records*, these two 15-year-olds were left nearly $415,000 in the early '60s from the estate of their owner, Dr. William Grier of San Diego.

Though technically, Hellcat and Brownie were two of the richest cat heirs, they did have to share their fortune. So, even better off than these two is Charlie Chan – a white alley cat who got to keep his $250,000 inheritance all to himself!

Why don't cats wash up before they eat?

The legend surrounding this behavior could well be described as the quick-witted mouse and the dimwitted cat.

As legend tells it, the cat once caught a mouse and was about to prepare the tasty little morsel when the mouse chided the cat for her bad manners. "What?" cried the mouse, "you're going to eat me without first washing your face and hands?" The mortified cat immediately dropped the mouse and began washing. And the clever little mouse promptly scooted off.

Ever since, cats have never washed up before dinner.

When Charlie Chan's owner, Mrs. Grace Alma Patterson, died in 1978, she left him a bounty that included a three-bedroom house, a seven-acre pet cemetery and a valuable antiques collection. When this wealthy puss dies, his estate will be auctioned off and the proceeds donated to local and national humane societies.

While it's true that no single kitty inherited Ben Rea's huge estate, thousands of anonymous cats' lives will be a whole lot better because of him. Rea, an eccentric bachelor, died at age 82, and left his fortune – a whopping $14 million – to three cat charities!

Who loves cats more – men or women?

Women have always been known as the most passionate cat lovers. Men, of course, love them, too; but they don't seem to get quite as nuts over cats.

This 'women love cats more' theory may have roots in our own cultural biology: Since way back in prehistoric times, men banded together and survived based on their group hunting instinct. So, even today, they don't identify with the single hunter – the cat. More than likely, men will prefer animals that are group hunters – like dogs.

Also, because women probably spend more time and attention on cats than men do, it appears that cats respond more to women. Of course, this isn't so. Cats are completely gender-neutral. In our household, two of our kitties adore my husband so much that they actually insist on being carried around by him, like newborn babies.

How big was the biggest cat?

Some cats don't need their hair standing on end to make them appear big. They are big!

Considering that the average cat weighs about 12 pounds, more or less, just try and picture some of these:

The heaviest cat on record was Himmy, an Australian cat who weighed a whopping 45 pounds, 10 ounces. He was the *Guinness Book of Records*' official world heavyweight champ in 1986.

Himmy's weight broke the record of the previous title-holder: Spice, a ginger-and-white tom from Ridgefield, CT, weighed 43 pounds when she died in 1977.

The *Toronto Star* newspaper reported that Boots, a black-and-white alley cat weighed 53 pounds – the fattest ever. But Boots' weight was never officially confirmed, so she never made it into *Guinness*.

Where is Weight Watchers when you need them?

What is the greatest number of mice killed by a cat?

How does 28,899 strike you? Pretty impressive, I'd say. The magnificent mouser who performed this feat was Towser, a tortoise-shell tabby who was in charge of rodent control at the Glenturret Distillery Ltd. in Scotland.

Towser, of course, had quite a long time to accomplish all her mousing – she lived to be 21. But this doesn't minimize her prize-winning performance. That's about four mice a day – every day – until she died in 1987!

Where did the name pussy willow come from?

This type of plant has the same name throughout the world (in different languages, of course); and the name may have come from the following Polish legend:

Long ago, a mother cat was crying on the bank of a river in which her kittens were drowning. The willows at the river's edge longed to help her, so they swept their long graceful branches into the water in order to rescue the tiny kittens. Gripping on tightly, the kittens were brought safely to shore. Every springtime since, says the tale, the willow branches bring forth their tiny buds at the tips, where the kittens originally clung. And those buds have the same silky feel as a kitten's soft fur.

Which cat was
the most famous
movie star?

If Hollywood actresses complain there aren't enough good movie roles for women, imagine what a cat-starlet might say! There generally haven't been a whole lot of major film roles for felines and most of those go to males.

My personal favorite was Tonto, the self-possessed cat who accompanied the curmudgeonly character, played Oscar-winningly by Art Carney, in the 1974 film, *Harry and Tonto*. As they crossed the country like two vagabond travelers, Tonto tolerated all their misadventures with unflinching good grace.

Who was the best
known cat of recent
times?

That title goes to Morris, the red tabby who really needs no introduction.

But did you know about his rags-to-riches story? Morris actually was discovered – hungry and weak – in a stray-animal shelter before he began advertising 9-Lives cat food. It was those wonderful commercials that made him a *numero uno* celebrity.

In 1973, Morris won an award as Best Animal Actor in TV commercials, and even had a biography published. He died in 1978.

A long search for his successor resulted in Morris the Second, also found in a shelter and who is now just as famous as the original. He works about 20 days a year filming his commercials and flies first-class all over the United States in support of adopt-a-pet programs. What a success story!

Should we even ask about the cat haters?

They are called ailurophobes, from the Greek *ailouros,* which means 'tail waver'.

Among the most famous cat haters were Julius Caesar, Adolph Hitler, Napoleon and Mussolini. Any surprises here? I didn't think so.

One that may surprise you though was Dwight D. Eisenhower. The famed World War II general and President of the United States was also famous for his cat hating. He even issued orders to the staff at his Gettysburg home that any cats seen on the grounds were to be shot. Who voted for this guy anyway?

Which famous folks were cat lovers?

Winston Churchill was so devoted to Jock, his ginger tomcat, that he let him sleep in his bed and even brought him to all the wartime cabinet meetings.

Mohammed's cat, Muezza, once fell asleep on the sleeve of the prophet's robe. When Mohammed was called to prayer, he decided to cut the sleeve off the robe rather than wake the cat.

Dr. Albert Schweitzer, who was awarded the Nobel Peace Prize in 1952, actually became ambidextrous (equally able to use both right and left hand) because of his cat, Sizi. The good doctor was left-handed, but when Sizi would fall asleep on his left arm, he would begin writing prescriptions with his right hand. Maybe that was the start of unreadable handwriting among doctors.

Did any American president besides Bill Clinton ever have a cat?

Certainly Socks is the kitty of the day – and it's high time that a cat got all that attention, wouldn't you say? But Socks wasn't quite the first.

Actually, the first White House cat came even before there was a White House. Before becoming the first First Lady, Martha Washington, wife of our first president, kept cats at Mount Vernon and even installed a special kitty door for them.

Teddy Roosevelt was also a great cat lover. His White House cat was named Tom Quartz, and there's even a biography written about him – the cat, that is.

And one presidential cat holds a dual distinction: Rutherford B. Hayes' cat not only was lucky enough to be a White House cat, but was also the first Siamese ever introduced into the United States, the gift of a foreign notable.

Why do cats develop the habit of sucking wool?

Boredom, loneliness and nutritional deficiencies all have been suggested as root causes of this bizarre behavior – which could end up ruining your entire winter wardrobe!

Most experts, however, agree that the reason for this behavior is pretty easy to zero in on. When your kitty settles down onto a nice wool blanket or your angora sweater, her movements are identical to those of a tiny nursing kitten: She presses her mouth against the soft wool, gnaws or sucks in pleasure, and 'kneads' against it...just like a kitten does to stimulate her mother's milk flow. However, this kitten-like behavior in older cats is somewhat unusual, say cat experts. It can indicate, they say, that the animal may have been orphaned or deprived too soon of her mother's care. It's something like thumb-sucking in children beyond a reasonable age.

If this behavior persists, it can become a problem. Loose strands from the prolonged sucking can be swallowed and eventually could block Kitty's intestines. The next step might be a vet visit – and maybe even surgery. But basically, the behavior is harmless.

Why do the pupils of a cat's eyes shrink from circles to vertical slits?

The rounded pupils of your cat's eyes reduce in size for the same reason that all animals' eyes do: to cut down on the amount of light that enters them. In your cat, this handy feature helps protect the particularly sensitive layer of cells that cover the retina from overexposure to light.

Wouldn't it seem more logical, though, that rounded pupils would shrink into smaller circles, like ours do? I sure think so. So what's with the slit bit?

Here again, it's nature's way of giving your kitty a unique advantage. Not even lions' eyes can do what your cat's eyes do. Like ours, a lion's eyes contract only to pinpricks. This is just fine for lions because they're daytime killers.

Kitty, however, is a night stalker. And because her eyes are so incredibly sensitive, she can see just fine in dim light. So very bright light would dazzle her. Her pupils become vertical so that she can use the closing of her lids to control the light input even further. If her pupils shrunk just to tiny dots, her half-closed eyes would block out light altogether. If you want to figure out the geometry, her pupils work at right angles to her eyelids. In this way, she can make the most delicate adjustments when exposed to what otherwise could be blinding light.

Do cats ever get lonely?

Far too many cat owners think of a cat as an object that falls somewhere between a piece of furniture and a wind-up toy. They assume that because cats are so independent, they don't really need our company. Nothing could be further from the truth.

Sure, most cats can get along just fine and dandy on their own – for a while. But many would rather have human companionship, and actually come to depend on having us around. Besides, there's a pretty big difference between alone and lonely.

It's a common mistake that cats don't much care for company. In the wild, it may be true that they're solitary creatures, and only seek out other cats to fight or to mate; but even in the wild, they enjoy the company of other cats.

Cats really are natural companions and have adapted remarkably well to sharing their lives with us – even if yours only hangs around because she loves getting all that TLC from you!

One of my cats, Little Guy, craves human companionship and attention so much that he makes a perpetual nuisance of himself in his never-ending pursuit of our affection.

Owners who leave their cats for long absences wind up creating lots of lonely kitties. For these cats, being alone results in a nerve-wracking boredom – and ultimately in the sort of real loneliness that can create a warped personality. Your cat may show signs of her unhappiness by grooming herself excessively; and even might literally chew her tail to shreds.

It's not even unusual for lonely cats to make themselves sick – which is one way of getting your attention. They're not faking it, though; they really are ill. The illness simply stems from emotional problems brought on by loneliness.

Some folks think a turned-on TV set is a good substitute for quality time with Kitty. Save the electricity! A group of animal psychologists in Germany studied the effects of TV on pets and found that too much TV can actually cause a cat to become neurotic. It seems a cat who 'watches' more than one hour a day becomes nervous and loses her appetite.

Even if your cat doesn't *seem* to want your company, you can be sure she at least prefers the presence of *someone*. In fact, cats who are left alone less often are more gentle and well-adjusted. That's why two cats are better than one. Sure, you can distract her with toys, but she prefers YOU!

Which cat had the most unusual job?

Towser's mousing mission at the Scottish distillery certainly ranks as noteworthy. But it really wasn't so unusual. Many cats, after all, have held similar jobs: Mike, for instance, was a loyal and punctual mouser at the British Museum for two decades, 1909 to 1929. Mike did have the distinction, however, of actually getting paid for his work. Sir Ernest Wallis Budge, the Museum's eminent Egyptologist and Keeper of Egyptian and Assyrian Antiquities (what a mouthful!) contributed sixpence a week to Mike's upkeep.

Among the really weird working cats, though, is the one who unfortunately remains nameless in the feline history books. What does remain, however, is the result of her enormous efforts. You could say this anonymous kitty actually helped build the Grand Coulee Dam!

When engineers were building the dam, they ran into some trouble threading a cable through a pipe. Someone suggested this supple solution: the flexible cat. So the engineers tied a rope to the thick misbehaving cable, then tied a slender string to the rope – and finally hitched the string to the tail of the cat. Our nameless hero expertly crawled through the labyrinthine pipeline and successfully finished the job.

Whatever induced the kitty to thread her way through that pipe? The record books don't say. But I suspect mouse fragrance may have played a part.

What is cat therapy?

Despite what this sounds like, it isn't taking your cat to the couch. In this case, it's the cat who plays the leading role ... the cat as therapist, so to speak.

This is not to imply that we'll be reading a 'Dear Tabby' column anytime soon. But cat's can work miracles.

Professionals who work among the elderly, ill and emotionally disturbed, for example, are finding that cats and other pets can help improve the quality of life of these people. Frequently, the mood of a person placed in close contact with a cat improves dramatically. As a result, many forward-looking institutions are beginning to use cats routinely for this purpose.

There are several reasons for the great results: cats are an antidote to loneliness. They are capable of love and companionship, of establishing real satisfying relationships with humans and can give aging owners a new purpose and meaning in life.

There are zillions of stories about cats bringing people out of years of withdrawal just by their presence, like some sixth sense responding to their soft and silent nature.

Heaven knows, there are plenty of waiting laps.

Will my cat ever need a shrink?

What on earth, you may ask, would a cat have to be depressed about? Plenty!

Like humans, cats can have a midlife crises or get just plain stressed out. They can suffer from a wide range of nervous disorders, and may merit the help of your local kitty therapist to 'work' their problems out.

Mainly, they suffer from two types of problems: one stems from never having been exposed to an adequate range of experiences as kittens to help them cope with the array of challenges they have to face as grown-up cats. Problems like extremely withdrawn behavior can arise from insufficient habituation to human contact at an early age. And, poor cat will probably hide even when there's no real reason to flee, like from any noise or quick movement that scares the life out of him.

The second type of nervous disorder stems from your cat's sudden loss of her ability to cope with particular experiences, like the arrival of a stranger into your home. This reaction can be caused by one unpleasant or frightening situation that now gets generalized; that's why it's important to make sure everyone who comes in contact with your cat does so in a positive way.

In either instance, you or a caring professional needs to make every attempt to understand not just why your cat is doing what she's doing but how to change her behavior.

But don't fret yet. *Newsweek* magazine recently reported on research that Prozac, the controversial mood-altering drug, is proving of some benefit to compulsive pets. After all, cats appear to exhibit some of the same compulsive behaviors as we do!

I wonder if cats are covered under national health care? Hopefully, President Clinton's cat, Socks, is taking care of that!